WORKBOOK

¡Viva el Español!

Ava Belisle-Chatterjee

Linda West Tibensky

Abraham Martínez-Cruz

National Textbook Company
a division of NTC/CONTEMPORARY PUBLISHING GROUP
Lincolnwood, Illinois USA

ISBN: 0-8442-0945-7

Published by National Textbook Company,
a division of NTC/Contemporary Publishing Group, Inc.
4255 West Touhy Avenue,
Lincolnwood (Chicago), Illinois 60712-1975 U.S.A.

0 1 2 3 4 5 6 7 8 VL 9 8 7 6 5

CONTENTS

¡BIENVENIDOS!

UNIDAD 1

UNIDAD 2

UNIDAD 3

REPASO
Unidades 1–3

UNIDAD 4

UNIDAD 5

¡Hablemos!   Nombre _____

A. You are the teacher and there are five new students in class. Find out what their names are. Write the answers on the lines below.

☐M **a.** ¿Cómo te llamas?

    b. Me llamo Carlos.

    Un muchacho se llama Carlos. _____

1. _____

2. _____

3. _____

4. _____

5. _____

B. You heard a conversation about Arturo, Rosa, and señorita Luisa. Unscramble the letters below the answer blank to form a word and complete each statement you heard.

☐M ¿Cómo se llama la ____**muchacha**____ ?
                        chamucha

1. Se _____ Rosa.
          malla

2. ¿ _____ se llama la señorita?
      omóc

3. Se llama _____ Luisa.
         ñosetari

4. El _____ se llama Arturo.
      chamucho

¡Hablemos!   Nombre _____

c. It's very noisy around school today. You can only hear one half of each conversation. What do you think the other person is saying? Choose the question or answer that should complete the conversation. Write its letter in the empty balloon.

a. ¿Cómo estás?
b. ¡Buenos días!
c. Me llamo Beto.
d. ¿Cómo te llamas?

f. ¿Cómo se llama el muchacho?
g. Muy bien, gracias.
h. ¡Buenas tardes!
i. ¡Hola!

¡Hablemos!   Nombre _____

D.   Andrés and María are trying to hold a conversation. Help them ⬚
the word that is missing. Write the word on the line.

| pronto | gracias | luego | llamo |
| Cómo | Buenas | √ Hola | días |

[M]   ANDRÉS: ¡ _____Hola_____ ! ¿Cómo estás?

1.   MARÍA: Buenos _____ .

2.   Bien, _____ .

3.   ANDRÉS: ¿ _____ te llamas?

4.   MARÍA: Me _____ María.

5.   ANDRÉS: Hasta _____ , María.

6.   MARÍA: Hasta _____ , Andrés.

E.   Someone has erased the punctuation marks on your page! Choose the
punctuation marks that go with each line. Then write the marks on the line.

[M]   LUIS: **¡Buenas tardes!** _____

1.   **Cómo te llamas** _____

2.   ELENA: **Buenas tardes** _____

3.   **Me llamo Elena** _____

4.   **Y tú cómo te llamas** _____

5.   LUIS: **Me llamo Luis** _____

6.   ELENA: **Adiós, Luis** _____

7.   LUIS: **Hasta pronto** _____

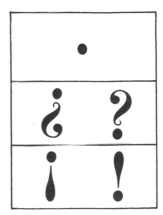

¡Hablemos!   Nombre _____

F.   You and your friends greet one another every day. To keep from getting bored, try to change greetings. Write at least one or two responses to each statement.

M   ¡Adiós!   **¡Hasta luego! ¡Hasta pronto!** _____

1. ¡Hola! _____

2. ¿Cómo estás? _____

3. ¡Hasta mañana!_____

_____

4. ¿Qué tal? _____

_____

THINK FAST! ∿∿∿∿∿∿∿∿∿∿∿∿∿

1. Circle the greeting you would use at 7:30 in the morning.

Buenas tardes.   Buenos días.   Buenas noches.

2. What do you say when someone asks you this question:

¿Cómo te llamas?

_____

3. Circle the answer you might give if someone asks you this question:

¿Cómo estás?

¡Hasta luego!   Se llama Juan.   Muy bien, gracias.

4. Circle the greeting you would use at 9:00 at night.

Buenas tardes.   Buenos días.   Buenas noches.

Nombre _____

La página de diversiones

1

¿Cómo está Benito?

El muchacho se llama Benito.

LA PROFESORA: ¿Cómo estás, Benito?

BENITO: Estoy muy mal. ¡Muy mal!

4

La página de diversiones

2

La muchacha se llama Carlota.

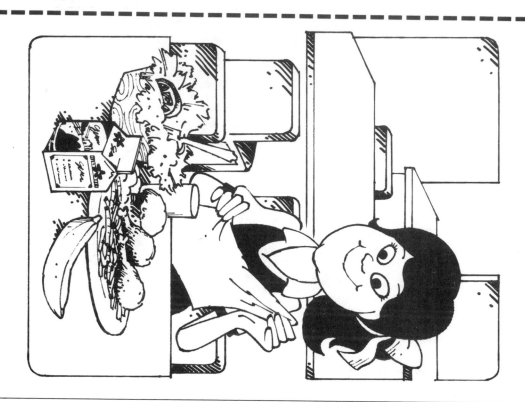

LA PROFESORA: ¿Cómo estás, Carlota?

CARLOTA: Estoy muy bien, gracias.

3

¡Hablemos!   Nombre _____

A.   Rosalía and Rodrigo are making a picture of their classroom. To check what they have included, write the number next to the correct word in the lists below. One has already been done for you.

M	**2** una luz		____ un escritorio
	____ una pizarra		____ una computadora
	____ la profesora		____ un pupitre
	____ una puerta		____ una silla

¡Hablemos!   Nombre _____

B. The teacher has decorated the bulletin board, but she forgot to connect the labels to the pictures. Draw a line from each picture to its label. One has been done for you. Trace over the dotted line.

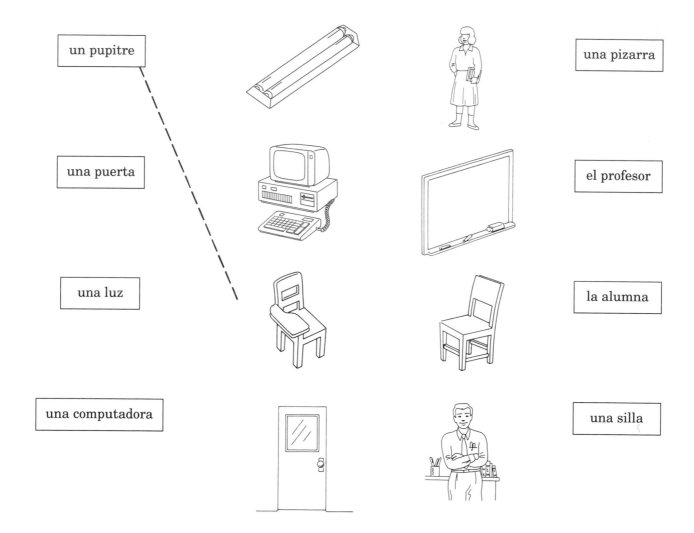

un pupitre		una pizarra
una puerta		el profesor
una luz		la alumna
una computadora		una silla

¡Hablemos! Nombre _____

C. Help Josefina finish the labels for her pictures. Read the sentence and write in the missing letters to complete the label.

Es un es __c__ __r__ __i__ torio.

1.

Es una ____ ____ zarra.

2.

Es un ____ ____ ____ bre.

3.

Es un a ____ ____ ____ no.

4.

Es una ____ ____ ll ____ .

5.

Es una mu ____ ____ ____ .

¡Hablemos!   Nombre _____

D. Paco wants to ask you about the classroom, but he doesn't always ask the right question. Help him out. Circle the letter of the question he should ask.

M Es una computadora.

   (a.) ¿Qué es esto?

   b. ¿Quién es?

1. Es una luz.

   a. ¿Qué es esto?

   b. ¿Quién es?

2. Es una alumna.

   a. ¿Qué es esto?

   b. ¿Quién es?

3. Es el profesor.

   a. ¿Qué es esto?

   b. ¿Quién es?

4. Es un escritorio.

   a. ¿Qué es esto?

   b. ¿Quién es?

5. Es un alumno.

   a. ¿Qué es esto?

   b. ¿Quién es?

6. Es un pupitre.

   a. ¿Qué es esto?

   b. ¿Quién es?

7. Es una silla.

   a. ¿Qué es esto?

   b. ¿Quién es?

8. Es la profesora.

   a. ¿Qué es esto?

   b. ¿Quién es?

¡Hablemos!   Nombre _____

E. Hortensia fell asleep in class and doesn't know all the words! How do you answer her questions? Write the answer to the question on the lines.

M  ¿Es un pupitre?

No, no es un pupitre.

M  ¿Es un escritorio?

Sí, es un escritorio.

1.  ¿Es la alumna?

_____

_____

2.  ¿Es una luz?

_____

_____

3.  ¿Es una silla?

_____

_____

4.  ¿Es un libro?

_____

_____

5.  ¿Es una pizarra?

_____

_____

6.  ¿Es la profesora?

_____

_____

THINK FAST! ∿∿∿∿∿∿∿∿∿∿∿∿∿∿∿∿

1. Name two things in the classroom that run on electricity.

_____

2. Name two things in the classroom that are pieces of furniture.

_____

¡Hablemos!   Nombre _____

F.   Draw your own classroom! Label each object or person next to its picture.

Nombre _____

La Página de diversiones

Busca las palabras

Read the words in the list and try to find them in the box. The words are either down or across. When you find a word, circle it and then make a check mark by the word in the list. One has been done for you.

alumna

el

la

luz

pizarra

puerta

pupitre

√ silla

un

una

S	I	L	L	A	Z	E	U	N
L	O	S	U	L	O	B	I	T
E	M	M	P	U	E	R	T	A
L	A	I	I	M	O	S	C	A
X	N	O	T	N	U	N	A	L
D	P	I	Z	A	R	R	A	U
P	U	P	I	T	R	E	U	Z

¡Hablemos!   Nombre _____

A. Your school received a shipment today. All the things must be counted before they are taken to the right rooms. Look at the picture and write the word or words for each number you see.

 M **siete**
_____
puertas

1.  _____
sillas

2.  _____
computadoras

3.  _____
pizarras

4.  _____
luces

5.  _____
pupitres

THiNK FAST! ∿∿∿∿∿∿∿∿∿∿∿∿∿∿

Circle the highest number in each row.

1. catorce   quince   trece   veinte

2. nueve   diez   siete   cuatro

3. dieciséis   dieciocho   diecisiete   once

4. dos   veintidós   doce   veintitrés

¡Hablemos!   Nombre _____

B.   Pepito's computer is broken. It has changed all the numerals of his addition problems into words. Change the words back into numbers.

M   Cuatro más uno son cinco.

   4 + 1 = 5
   _____

1. Diez más dos son doce.

   _____

2. Once más diez son veintiuno.

   _____

3. Trece más tres son dieciséis.

   _____

4. Siete más ocho son quince.

   _____

5. Nueve más catorce son veintitrés.

   _____

6. Uno más doce son trece.

   _____

7. Veinticuatro más dos son veintiséis.

   _____

8. Veintiocho más uno son veintinueve.

   _____

THINK FAST! 〰〰〰〰〰〰〰〰〰〰

How do you ask a classmate for his or her telephone number? Unscramble each word and write it in the answer blank.

¿ _____ es tu _____ de _____ ?
        áucl   úrenom   lootnefé

¡Hablemos!   Nombre _____

C. Luisa has called to ask you for the telephone numbers of some classmates. Before you read them to her, write down the words for each number.

M Víctor: 342-8732

tres, cuatro, dos—ocho, siete, tres, dos
_____

M Amalia: 921-1524

nueve, veintiuno—quince, veinticuatro
_____

1. Juanita: 863-5060

_____

2. Anselmo: 585-9864

_____

3. Timoteo: 765-8743

_____

4. Margarita: 713-2514

_____

5. Bernardo: 829-1618

_____

¡Hablemos!   Nombre _____

D.   Make your own telephone book! Ask ten classmates for their telephone
numbers. Then write down their names and numbers on the page.

Mis amigos

Nombre	Número de teléfono
1. _____	_____
2. _____	_____
3. _____	_____
4. _____	_____
5. _____	_____
6. _____	_____
7. _____	_____
8. _____	_____
9. _____	_____
10. _____	_____

Nombre _____

La Página de diversiones

Busca el número

Find the name of the number in each row. Draw a circle around the word that stands for the numeral on the left. Follow the model by tracing the circle.

7	tres	ocho	dos	(siete)	cuatro
5	cinco	tres	quince	seis	uno
12	ocho	dos	once	doce	siete
4	veinte	cuatro	diez	catorce	dos
13	nueve	tres	trece	cinco	uno

¿Qué número falta?

Write the number that is missing to make each problem correct.

M cinco más _____**cuatro**_____ son nueve

1. diez más _____ son quince

2. once más _____ son veinte

3. _____ más doce son veintiséis

4. _____ más cuatro son veintiuno

5. veintitrés más _____ son veintinueve

¡Hablemos!   Nombre _____

A. Claudia made a poster of her classroom. Unfortunately, the glue was old and many of the pictures fell off. Help her fix it. Read each sentence, then draw a line from the picture in the first column to the picture in the second column, according to the sentence. Follow the model by tracing over the dotted line.

M Hay un bolígrafo en el pupitre.

1. Hay un reloj en la pared.

2. Hay una hoja de papel en el escritorio.

3. Hay un globo en la mesa.

4. Hay una regla en la silla.

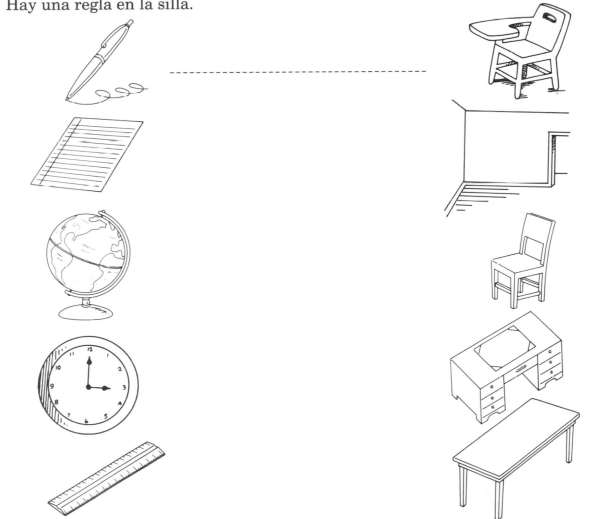

¡Hablemos!   Nombre _____

B. Gregorio is writing words on the chalkboard. Every time he moves to the next word, his sleeve erases part of another word. Help him out. Write the missing letters in the blank spaces to complete the words. (Note: There are more words in the list than you will need!)

el pupitre   el borrador   el mapa
la pared   el globo   la luz
la tiza   √ la cesta   la mesa

M   la __c__ __e__ sta.

1. la ____ ____ sa.   4. el borra ____ ____ ____

2. la pa ____ ____ d.   5. la ____ ____ za

3. el ____ ____ pa   6. el pupi ____ ____ ____

THINK FAST! ∿∿∿∿∿∿∿∿∿∿∿∿∿∿∿∿∿∿

Circle the largest object in each row. Draw a box around the smallest object in each row.

1.   el borrador   la ventana   el reloj

2.   el pupitre   el globo   la tiza

3.   la tiza   el mapa   la puerta

4.   la mesa   la cesta   la pared

¡Hablemos!   Nombre _____

C. Mario has a messy desk! How in the world can he fit so many things in his desk? On the line beside each number, write the name of the object with that number on it. The first one is done for you.

¿Qué hay en el pupitre?

1. __el globo_____   5. _____

2. _____   6. _____

3. _____   7. _____

4. _____

¿Cómo lo dices?   Nombre _____

A. Julia needs your help. She doesn't know how to change the words in her list to show more than one. Circle the ending you would add to each word and write the word in the blank.

M	mujer	s	(es)	**mujeres** _____
1.	hombre	s	es	_____
2.	reloj	s	es	_____
3.	pared	s	es	_____
4.	pupitre	s	es	_____
5.	papel	s	es	_____

THINK FAST!

Now that you know the endings that can help you talk about more than one object, you can recognize the endings on unfamiliar words, too.

Look at the following pairs of words. Draw a circle around the word that stands for more than one object. Draw a box around the word that stands for one object.

1.   tocador   tocadores

2.   carteles   cartel

3.   enchufes   enchufe

4.   billete   billetes

UNIDAD 1

¿Cómo lo dices?   Nombre _____

B. Sergio is preparing a report about his classroom. Help him finish his sentences. Choose the word you would use to complete the sentence and write the word in the blank.

M   Hay tres _____**borradores**_____ en el salón de clase.

borrador   (borradores)

1. Hay diez _____ .

profesor   profesores

2. Hay un _____ en la _____ .

reloj   relojes   pared   paredes

3. Los _____ son _____ .

profesor   profesores   hombre   hombres

4. Las _____ son _____ .

profesora   profesoras   mujer   mujeres

C. How well can you talk about more than one thing? Decide whether you would use **s** or **es** to talk about more than one. Write the word in the blank.

M      un televisor

dos __**televisores**__

1.    un actor

dos _____

2.   un títere

dos _____

3.   un sol

dos _____

¿Cómo lo dices?   Nombre _____

D. How well do you know your own classroom? Count the number of objects or people. Then write the answer.

M ¿Cuántos mapas hay en el salón de clase?

Hay dos mapas. _____

1. ¿Cuántas mesas hay en el salón de clase?

_____

2. ¿Cuántas alumnas hay en el salón de clase?

_____

3. ¿Cuántos borradores hay en la pizarra?

_____

4. ¿Cuántos pupitres hay en el salón de clase?

_____

5. ¿Cuántos bolígrafos hay en los pupitres?

_____

6. ¿Cuántas paredes hay en el salón de clase?

_____

7. ¿Cuántas ventanas hay en la puerta?

_____

8. ¿Cuántos relojes hay en el salón de clase?

_____

¿Cómo lo dices?   Nombre _____

E. It's "Visitors' Night" at school and you have been assigned the task of making labels for items in the classroom. Write the word **el, los, la,** or **las** in the label.

M
       el
      _____
      cuaderno

1.
      _____
      ventanas

2.
      _____
      globo

3.
      _____
      bolígrafo

4.
      _____
      escritorios

5.
      _____
      cestas

6.
      _____
      regla

¿Cómo lo dices?　　　Nombre _____

F. As tour guide for Visitors' Night, you are in charge of answering people's questions. Write the answer in the blanks.

M  ¿Qué es esto?

Es __**la mesa**__

_____ .

1.  ¿Qué son estos?

Son _____

_____ .

2.  ¿Qué es esto?

Es _____

_____ .

3.  ¿Qué son estos?

Son _____

_____ .

4.  ¿Quién es?

Es _____

_____ .

5.  ¿Quién es?

Es _____

_____ .

6.  ¿Qué es esto?

Es _____

_____ .

7.  ¿Quién es?

Es _____

_____ .

8. 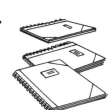 ¿Qué son estos?

Son _____

_____ .

¿Cómo lo dices?   Nombre _____

G.   Some people at Visitors' Night want to speak Spanish, but they need help. Look at the pictures, read the questions, and then complete the sentences.

M   ¿Es la mesa?

No, no es la mesa. Es el pupitre.

1.   ¿Son las alumnas?

No, no son _____

2.   ¿Es la tiza?

No, no es _____

3.   ¿Son los cuadernos?

No, no son _____

4.   ¿Son los bolígrafos?

No, no son _____

5.   ¿Es la bandera?

No, no es _____

¿Cómo lo dices?   Nombre _____

H. You and your friends are playing "Find the Question." For each answer, find the right question from the box. Then write it on the line above the answer.

¿Qué es esto?	¿Quién es?
¿Qué son estos?	¿Quiénes son?

M **¿Quién es?**
_____

Es el profesor.

4. _____

Son los pupitres.

1. _____

Es un amigo.

5. _____

Son Rogelio y Susana.

2. _____

Son los lápices.

6. _____

Es un libro.

3. _____

Es el salón de clase.

7. _____

Son las alumnas.

¿Cómo lo dices?   Nombre _____

¡APRENDE MÁS!

The Spanish alphabet is almost like the one you know in English. The sounds that the letters stand for are not the same. But in most cases, the letters are written the same way.

One of the letters stands for a special sound. This letter is different from the ones you know. Look at the alphabet below and circle the letter that is different.

El alfabeto en español

A, a	H, h	Ñ, ñ	U, u
B, b	I, i	O, o	V, v
C, c	J, j	P, p	W, w
D, d	K, k	Q, q	X, x
E, e	L, l	R, r	Y, y
F, f	M, m	S, s	Z, z
G, g	N, n	T, t	

Nombre _____

La página de diversiones

Busca las palabras

Read the words in the list and try to find them in the box. The words are either down or across. When you find a word, circle it and then make a check by the word in the list. One has been done for you.

bolígrafo
cuaderno
libro

regla
✓ papel
reloj

lápiz
cesta
globo

bandera
mapa
pared

C	E	S	T	A	V	L	A	P	I	Z	R
O	M	R	Z	P	U	T	R	A	H	X	E
L	G	O	A	S	M	R	T	P	B	J	L
L	L	E	V	C	U	A	D	E	R	N	O
Y	O	P	A	S	H	E	C	L	E	O	J
U	B	Y	V	W	U	B	D	S	G	G	H
B	O	L	I	G	R	A	F	O	L	L	K
N	R	I	N	F	D	N	I	M	A	Z	Q
T	S	B	G	W	Y	D	Z	Q	R	K	L
S	E	R	P	A	R	E	D	E	R	L	O
U	I	O	K	Q	A	R	I	F	Z	X	I
Z	O	I	M	A	P	A	K	W	Q	C	U

¡Hablemos!   Nombre _____

A. Rita drew a picture for her math class, but now she needs to count how many geometric shapes she drew to make Maqui, the robot. Answer the questions.

1. ¿Cuántos cuadrados hay?   _____

2. ¿Cuántos círculos hay?   _____

3. ¿Cuántos rectángulos hay?   _____

4. ¿Cuántos triángulos hay?   _____

UNIDAD 2

B. You have entered a contest. If you unscramble the letters and write all the words correctly, you will win. Start now!

M El flamenco es **rosado** .

odsaro

1. El ratón es _____ .

isgr

2. El canario es _____ .

riamallo

3. El oso es _____ .

ogner

4. El loro es _____ .

devre

¡Hablemos!   Nombre _____

C. Pepito is showing you his coloring book. What can you say about the picture? Color in the picture, then answer the questions.

M ¿Cómo es Antonio?

Antonio es grande.

1. ¿De qué color es el tigre?

_____

2. ¿De qué color es Pepe?

_____

3. ¿Qué animal es Raúl?

_____

4. ¿Qué animal es el profesor?

_____

5. ¿De qué color es Marcos?

_____

6. ¿Cómo es Raúl?

_____

7. ¿Cómo es Pepe?

_____

8. ¿Cómo es el señor Flamenco?

_____

¿Cómo lo dices?   Nombre _____

A.   Juanito has written some sentences about his classroom, but he isn't sure about how to write the descriptive words. Help him out. Use the descriptive word in parentheses to complete the sentence. Be sure to write the appropriate form of the word!

M   Las reglas son _____**largas**_____ . (largo)

1.   El escritorio es _____ . (pequeño)

2.   La puerta es _____ . (blanco)

3.   Los bolígrafos son _____ . (negro)

4.   Las sillas son _____ . (azul)

5.   La ventana es _____ . (grande)

6.   Las pizarras son _____ . (verde)

7.   Las cestas son _____ . (amarillo)

8.   Los cuadernos son _____ . (anaranjado)

THINK FAST! ∿∿∿∿∿∿∿∿∿∿∿∿∿

Circle the word in each row that does not belong.

1.   perro   tigre   oso   pez   azul

2.   loro   amarillo   rojo   gris   rosado

3.   triángulo   cuadrado   pequeño   rectángulo   círculo

4.   largo   corto   grande   ratón   pequeño

UNIDAD 2

B.   There are colors all around you. How many can you name? Complete the sentence by writing the color or colors of the classroom object.

M   El lápiz es   **negro y amarillo** _____ .

1.   La pizarra es _____ .

2.   Los pupitres son _____ .

3.   El cuaderno es _____ .

4.   La tiza es _____ .

C.   You're on your own! Make up your own sentences about items in your classroom. You may use colors or other words to describe them.

1. _____

2. _____

3. _____

4. _____

5. _____

UNIDAD 2

D. While you were helping señor Millones clean the attic, you found some treasures. What is in the attic? After looking at each picture, complete the sentence by writing **un, unos, una,** or **unas** in the blank.

M      Hay ___una___

bandera.

1.      Hay _____

oso.

2.      Hay _____

ratones.

3.      Hay _____

computadoras.

4.      Hay _____

globos.

5.      Hay _____

círculos.

6.      Hay _____

cesta.

THINK FAST!

How would you answer this question: **¿Cuál es tu animal favorito?**

_____

_____

¿Cómo lo dices?   Nombre _____

E.   Marta is feeling contrary today. If you see one thing, she sees more of
them. If you see some things, she only sees one. For each statement, write
the statement that Marta would say.

M   Hay una ventana grande.

MARTA: **Hay unas ventanas grandes.** _____

1.   Hay un loro verde y azul.

MARTA: _____

2.   Hay unos ratones pequeños.

MARTA: _____

3.   Hay unas computadoras blancas.

MARTA: _____

4.   Hay un círculo negro y un rectángulo morado.

MARTA: _____

5.   Hay una mariposa negra y azul.

MARTA: _____

6.   Hay un globo grande y unas reglas cortas.

MARTA: _____

¿Cómo lo dices?　　　Nombre _____

F. The animals from señora Luna's science class have escaped. Where are they now? For each picture, write a question and an answer. (Note: **P** means **Pregunta** or "Question" and **R** means **Respuesta** or "Answer.")

P: **¿Qué hay en el pupitre?** _____

R: **Hay unos loros en el pupitre.** _____

1.

P: _____

R: _____

2.

P: _____

R: _____

3. 　

P: _____

R: _____

4.

P: _____

R: _____

¿Cómo lo dices?   Nombre _____

¡APRENDE MÁS!

Once you know the alphabet in Spanish, you know how to put words in alphabetical order. And once you know alphabetical order, you will know how to look up words in a dictionary or glossary.

Let's practice. Each list of words is all mixed up. Next to the list, write the words in alphabetical order. (You do not need to know the meaning of a word to put it in order.) The first list has been started for you.

El alfabeto: a, b, c, d, e, f, g, h, i, j, k, l, m, n, ñ, o, p, q, r, s, t, u, v, w, x, y, z

1. silla   **alumno** _____   **3.** día   _____

   libro   _____   mañana   _____

   alumno   _____   luego   _____

   llueve   _____   noche   _____

2. computadora   _____   **4.** verde   _____

   pizarra   _____   una   _____

   escritorio   _____   reloj   _____

   corto   _____   ¿qué?   _____

Nombre _____

La Página de diversiones

Busca las palabras secretas

In each box there is one word that does not belong. Find the word and circle it. Then write the words in the blanks below to make a sentence.

1.

negro	rojo	amarillo
azul	rosado	perro
blanco	morado	verde

2.

loro	canario	tigre
ratón	pez	oso
gris	mariposa	pájaro

El _____ es _____ .

Now draw a picture to illustrate the secret animal.

¡Hablemos!   Nombre _____

A. What day does each date come on? Look at the calendar in exercise C, page 43. Find the date and write the name of the day on the blank beside it.

[M] 24   **jueves** _____

1. 2 _____   6. 5 _____

2. 18 _____   7. 29 _____

3. 27 _____   8. 11 _____

4. 14 _____   9. 3 _____

5. 10 _____   10. 30 _____

THiNK FAST! ∿∿∿∿∿∿∿∿∿∿∿∿∿∿∿∿∿

Look at each picture. Below the picture, write the day of the week on which you might go to the place or use the object.

1.

2.

3.

_____   _____   _____

4.

5.

6.

_____   _____   _____

¡Hablemos!   Nombre _____

B. Antonio goes to school on weekdays, but he always stays at home on the weekends. After reading the name of the day, write either **la escuela** or **la casa** in the blank.

M	martes	la escuela

1. jueves   _____

2. sábado   _____

3. lunes   _____

4. domingo   _____

5. viernes   _____

6. miércoles   _____

THiNK FAST! ∿∿∿∿∿∿∿∿∿∿∿∿∿∿

What day comes before each of these days?

1. lunes   _____

2. sábado   _____

3. jueves   _____

4. domingo   _____

¡Hablemos!   Nombre _____

C. Imagine that today is the fifteenth of the month. The date has been circled on your calendar. For each date listed, check the calendar. Write in the blank next to the date whether it is **esta semana** or **la próxima semana**.

lunes	martes	miércoles	jueves	viernes	sábado	domingo
	1	2	3	4	5	6
7	8	9	10	11	12	13
14	(15)	16	17	18	19	20
21	22	23	24	25	26	27
28	29	30				

M 24 __**la próxima semana**_____

1. 17 _____   4. 20 _____

2. 23 _____   5. 16 _____

3. 27 _____   6. 21 _____

A. Poor Lupita has a cold and can't hear well. Show her what each person is saying by completing the sentence that goes with the picture. Use **a la** or **al**.

M 

Voy __a la__ escuela.

1.

¿Vas _____ parque?

2.

¿Vas _____ cine?

¿Cómo lo dices?   Nombre _____

3.

Voy _____ casa.

4.

Voy _____ tienda.

B. You are trying to plan your activities for the week. How do your friends answer your questions? Write **voy, vas,** or **va** in the blank to complete the answer.

M ¿Va Jaime a la escuela hoy?

Sí, Jaime __va__ a la escuela.

1. ¿Vas a la escuela el martes?

Sí, _____ a la escuela.

2. ¿Va Isabel al cine esta semana?

No, no _____ al cine.

3. Voy a la escuela el domingo?

No, no _____ a la escuela.

4. ¿Va Luis al salón de clase?

Sí, _____ al salón de clase.

5. ¿Vas a la escuela el sábado?

No, no _____ a la escuela.

6. ¿Voy al parque el miércoles?

No, no _____ al parque.

THINK FAST! ∿∿∿∿

¿Qué día es hoy?

Hoy es _____.

C. Your male friends are going to the park this week. Your female friends are going to the park next week. Read the name in parentheses. Then, write a sentence about when that person is going to the park.

[M] (Jorge)   **Jorge va al parque esta semana.** _____

1. (Luisa)   _____

2. (Manuel)   _____

3. (Paco)   _____

4. (Elena)   _____

D. Where are your classmates going? Choose a question to ask four classmates, then ask them the question. Write a sentence about each person's answer.

Preguntas

1. ¿Vas al cine esta semana?
2. ¿Vas a la clase hoy?
3. ¿Vas a la tienda el fin de semana?

[M]   TÚ: ¿Vas al cine esta semana?
       JOSÉ: No, no voy al cine esta semana.

José no va al cine esta semana. _____

1. _____

2. _____

3. _____

4. _____

UNIDAD 3

¿Cómo lo dices?   Nombre _____

E. Javier's mother can never remember on what days he goes different places. To help his mother, Javier has made a calendar. Read the calendar and the questions. Write the answers in the blanks.

lunes	martes	miércoles	jueves	viernes	sábado	domingo
la escuela	la escuela	la escuela	la escuela	la escuela	la casa	la casa
y		y	y	y	y	y
la clase de guitarra		la clase de guitarra	la casa de José	el parque	la casa de Marta	el cine

M ¿Cuándo va a la casa de José?

Va a la casa de José el jueves.

1. ¿Cuándo va a la escuela?

_____

2. ¿Cuándo va al cine?

_____

3. ¿Cuándo va al parque?

_____

4. ¿Cuándo va a la clase de guitarra?

_____

5. ¿Cuándo no va a la escuela?

_____

¿Cómo lo dices?   Nombre _____

F. Señorita Durango is from Argentina. She is very interested in the activities of students in North America. How do you answer her questions? Write an answer that is true for you.

[M] ¿Adónde vas los lunes?

Voy a la escuela los lunes.
_____

1. ¿Cuándo vas a la escuela?

_____

2. ¿Adónde vas los fines de semana?

_____

3. ¿Cuándo vas a la casa de un amigo o de una amiga?

_____

4. ¿Vas a la tienda los sábados?

_____

5. ¿Adónde vas la próxima semana?

_____

6. ¿Vas al parque los miércoles?

_____

THINK FAST! ∿∿∿∿∿∿∿∿∿∿∿∿∿∿∿

First, unscramble the letters to form a word. Then write each word in the blank to form a sentence.

Voy al _____ los _____ _____ _____ .
           uqepra   esnif   ed   amnase

¿Cómo lo dices? Nombre _____

G. Miguel has given you a copy of his schedule for this week. What questions can you ask him about his activities? Read Miguel's calendar. Write six questions you could ask him: three questions with **¿Adónde?** and three questions with **¿Cuándo?** Look at the questions in exercise F if you need help.

El calendario de Miguel						
lunes	martes	miércoles	jueves	viernes	sábado	domingo
la escuela y la clase de piano	la escuela	¡No hay clases! el cine: "Los flamencos de Miami"	la escuela y la clase de piano	la escuela y la casa de Inés	la casa de Paco y el parque	la casa y el cine: "El tigre grande"

1. _____

2. _____

3. _____

4. _____

5. _____

6. _____

UNIDAD 3

H. Choose a partner. Ask your partner where he or she is going each day of the week and complete the calendar.

lunes	
martes	
miércoles	
jueves	
viernes	
sábado	
domingo	

UNIDAD 3

Nombre _____

¡APRENDE MÁS!

Using the glossary or word list in a textbook is like using a dictionary. It has information to help you find the meaning of a word.

Muchas gracias.
  Thank you very much. (B)
grande   big (2)
la **gripe**   flu (7)
  Tengo la gripe.   I have the flu. (7)
gris   gray (2)
gustar   to like (5)
  Me gusta el libro.   I like the book. (5)
  Le gusta el verano.
    He/she likes summer. (5)
  ¿Qué te gusta hacer?
    What do you like to do? (6)

entry words

hay (*inf.: haber*)   there is, there are (1)
  ¿Cuántos...hay?
    How many...are there? (1)
  ¿Qué hay...?   What is there...? (1)
la **hermana**   sister (10)
las **hermanas**   sisters (10)
la **hermanastra**   stepsister (10)
el **hermanastro**   stepbrother (10)
el **hermano**   brother (10)
los **hermanos**
    brothers, brothers and sisters (10)
la **hija**   daughter (10)

Find the following information in your textbook's Spanish-English Word List.

1. What is the first word on page 238 that means "a place to sit"?   _____

2. On page 232, what does the abbreviation (*m.*) mean after the word **el arte**?   _____

3. What animal's name is on page 239?   _____

4. What day of the week is on page 234?   _____

5. How many days of the week can you find on page 236?   _____

6. What words on page 233 are places?   _____

7. Read page 231, then write down the unit in which the word **el hijo** is taught.   _____

8. What is the last expression on page 235 that describes the weather?   _____

Nombre _____

La página de diversiones

Un juego de los días

Write the missing days of the week in the squares. One day is already written for you. Use the letters as clues to fill in the other days.

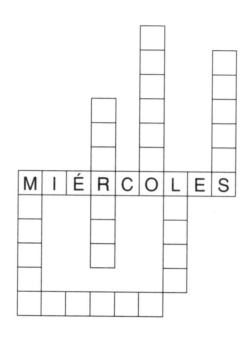

¿Adónde va el profesor?

First fill in the missing letter of each word. Then, complete the sentence by writing the word that is formed by the letters in the boxes.

```
        □ I N E
    M   □ R T E S
J U E V E □
    D Í □
```

El profesor va a la _____ .

Unidades 1–3   Nombre _____

A. Some objects in the classroom are out of place. Where do they go? Draw a line from each classroom object on the left to the picture of where it belongs. Then write the name of the picture in the blank. One has been done for you.

                                                  el cuaderno _____

una hoja de papel

unos bolígrafos

_____

el reloj

_____

el borrador

_____

una computadora

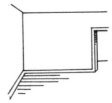

_____

Unidades 1–3   Nombre _____

B. How many are there? Read the sentence and the question. Then write the answer.

[M] Hay diez mesas largas y tres mesas cortas. ¿Cuántas mesas hay?

   Hay trece mesas.

---

1. Hay dos canarios y veinte loros. ¿Cuántos pájaros hay?

   _____

2. Hay cinco cuadrados blancos, cinco cuadrados azules y cinco cuadrados verdes. ¿Cuántos cuadrados hay?

   _____

3. Hay una pared blanca, una pared amarilla y dos paredes rosadas. ¿Cuántas paredes hay?

   _____

4. Hay diez gatos, siete perros y once peces. ¿Cuántos animales hay?

   _____

5. Hay diez hombres grandes y cuatro hombres pequeños. ¿Cuántos hombres hay?

   _____

6. Hay once profesores y quince profesoras. ¿Cuántos profesores hay?

   _____

REPASO

c.   Help Consuelo decorate the bulletin board! Find the picture that matches each sentence. Write the letter of the picture on the line beside the sentence. The first one has been done for you. (Look carefully! There are more pictures than there are sentences.)

1. Hay un calendario en la pared.   c
_____

2. El muchacho va al cine.   _____

3. La alumna va a la escuela.   _____

4. Hay dos ratones en el escritorio.   _____

5. Hay una mariposa en la ventana.   _____

6. Hay una computadora en el pupitre.   _____

a.  b.  c.  d.

e.  f.  g.  h.

Unidades 1–3   Nombre _____

D. Imagine that you are listening to one side of a telephone conversation. You can hear the answers but not the questions. Choose a question that goes with each answer and write it on the line. There are more questions than answers, so choose carefully!

¿Cuándo vas al parque?   ¿Qué día es hoy?
¿Cuál es tu animal favorito?   √ ¿Cómo te llamas?
¿Cómo estás?   ¿Adónde vas el viernes?
¿De qué color es tu perro?   ¿Cuándo vas a la escuela?
¿Cómo es la escuela?   ¿De qué color es el gato?
¿Cuál es tu número de teléfono? ¿Cuál es tu día favorito?

P: **¿Cómo te llamas?**
_____

R: Me llamo Patricio.

1. P: _____

R: Bien, gracias.

2. P: _____

R: Hoy es sábado.

3. P: _____

R: Voy al parque el domingo.

4. P: _____

R: Voy a la escuela el lunes.

5. P: _____

R: La escuela es grande.

6. P: _____

R: Mi animal favorito es el gato.

7. P: _____

R: El gato es gris, blanco y marrón oscuro.

8. P: _____

R: Mi número de teléfono es el tres, veinte, quince, cero, uno.

THINK FAST! ∿∿∿∿∿∿∿∿∿∿∿∿∿∿

1. Name three classroom objects you can hold in your hand.

_____   _____   _____

2. Write a number from 1 to 4 next to each animal. Rank the animals from the smallest (1) to the largest (4).

_____ conejo   _____ mariposa   _____ tigre   _____ pez

3. Write the names of five animals that can fly.

_____   _____

_____   _____

_____

4. Name two classroom objects you can put in your pocket.

_____   _____

5. Write an addition problem whose answer is your age.

_____ + _____ = _____

E. The local movie theater is taking a survey to find out about people who go to the movies. How do you answer the questions? Write answers that are true for you. Try to write complete sentences.

Cine Popular

1. ¿Cómo te llamas? _____

2. ¿Cuál es tu número de teléfono? _____

3. ¿Qué día es hoy? _____

4. ¿Vas al cine hoy? _____

5. ¿Vas al cine esta semana? _____

6. ¿Vas al cine la próxima semana? _____

   _____

7. ¿Vas al cine los fines de semana? _____

   _____

8. Generalmente, ¿qué día de la semana vas al cine? _____

   _____

9. ¿Vas al cine con un amigo o con una amiga? _____

   _____

10. ¿Cómo se llama tu amigo o tu amiga? _____

    _____

¡Hablemos!   Nombre _____

A. Where is Amalia going today? FInd the name of the class or place and write it on the lines beside the picture. (Be alert! There are more places than pictures.)

la clase de música   el cine
la clase de computadoras   la clase de arte
la biblioteca   ✓ la escuela
el gimnasio   la casa

M

la escuela
_____
_____

1.
_____
_____

2.
_____
_____

3.
_____
_____

4.
_____
_____

5.
_____
_____

¡Hablemos!   Nombre _____

B.   Your typewriter is broken! None of the vowels will print. Fill in the missing
letters on the labels beside each picture. One word has been done for you.

1.

___ s ___ r   l ___

c ___ mp ___ t ___ d ___ r ___

2.

c ___ nt ___ r

3.

___ st ___ d ___ ___ r

4.

pr ___ ct ___ c ___ r   l ___ s

d ___ p ___ rt ___ s

5.

p ___ nt ___ r

¡Hablemos!   Nombre _____

C. Gregorio has written a paragraph about school. When he didn't know a word, he drew a picture. Help him write the words on the lines below. The first one has been done for you.

Los lunes, los miércoles y los viernes voy a (**1**)

Voy a (**2**)  .   El martes voy al gimnasio para

(**3**)  .   El jueves voy a (**4**)    en

(**5**) 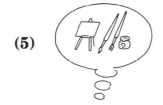 .   También voy a cantar en (**6**)

1. **la biblioteca** _____

2. _____

3. _____

4. _____

5. _____

6. _____

¿Cómo lo dices?   Nombre _____

A. Some of your friends want to know what they are scheduled to do this afternoon. How do you answer their questions? Write your answer below each question.

M

¿Qué voy a hacer?

Vas a pintar.
_____

1.

¿Qué va a hacer Marina?
_____

2.

¿Qué voy a hacer?
_____

3.

David, ¿qué vas a hacer?
_____

4.

¿Qué voy a hacer?
_____

¿Cómo lo dices?   Nombre _____

B. All day long Hortensia has been passing you notes in class. How do you answer her? Write your answers on the blanks.

M ¿Qué vas a hacer en el gimnasio?

Voy a practicar los deportes. _____

1. ¿Qué vas a hacer en la biblioteca?

_____

2. ¿Qué vas a hacer en la clase de arte?

_____

3. ¿Qué vas a hacer en la clase de computadoras?

_____

4. ¿Qué vas a hacer en la clase de música?

_____

THINK FAST! ∿∿∿∿∿∿∿∿∿∿∿∿∿

First, read and complete each sentence. Then complete the secret sentence with the letters you have written in the circles.

1. Hoy es miércoles. Mañana es ☐ ☐ ☐ ◯ ☐ ☐ .

2. La ☐ ◯ ☐ ☐ ☐ ☐ ☐ es un animal pequeño

    de muchos colores.

3. El muchacho ◯ ☐ llama Alberto.

    ¡ _____ _____ _____ a estudiar mucho!

C. Now Hortensia has written you a note about what she and her friend are going to do on Saturday. She wrote it so quickly that she forgot some words! To complete the note, write the appropriate form of **ir a**.

¡Hola!

El sábado [M] _____voy a_____ ir al cine. Mi amiga Olga

(1) _____ ir al cine también.

Olga (2) _____ estudiar el sábado.

El sábado no (3) _____ estudiar. No

(4) _____ ir a la biblioteca.

¿Qué (5) _____ hacer el sábado?

(6) ¿ _____ ir al cine con unos amigos?

¡Hasta luego!

Hortensia

UNIDAD 4

D. Little Paquito doesn't understand what you do in school. How do you answer his questions? Write your answers on the blanks.

M ¿Cantas en la clase de arte?

No, no canto en la clase de arte. _____

1. ¿Qué haces en la clase de arte?

_____

2. ¿Practicas los deportes en la biblioteca?

_____

3. ¿Qué haces en la biblioteca?

_____

4. ¿Usas la computadora en la clase de música?

_____

5. ¿Qué haces en la clase de música?

_____

¿Cómo lo dices?   Nombre _____

E. You took a picture of señora Jiménez's study group. Now you must write captions for the picture. Answer the questions below.

M ¿Qué hace Óscar?   **Óscar canta.** _____

1. ¿Qué hace Julio? _____

2. ¿Qué hace Elena? _____

3. ¿Qué hace Rosita? _____

4. ¿Qué hace Carlos? _____

UNIDAD 4

F.   You need to practice asking questions. You want to be a reporter someday. First, read the words to form the question. Then read the answer.

M   P: Eduardo / estudiar / dónde

¿Dónde estudia Eduardo?

R: Eduardo estudia en el salón de clase.

1. P: Nélida / cantar / cuándo

_____

R: Nélida canta los domingos.

2. P: el señor López / pintar / dónde

_____

R: El señor López pinta en la casa.

3. P: Minerva / la computadora / usar / cuándo

_____

R: Minerva usa la computadora los lunes.

4. P: la señora Ruiz / los deportes / practicar / dónde

_____

R: La señora Ruiz practica los deportes en el gimnasio.

¿Cómo lo dices?　　　Nombre _____

G. Señor Rodríguez thinks that everyone has a special talent. How will you fill out his questionnaire? Write an answer that is true for you.

M ¿Practicas los deportes en la escuela?

Sí, practico los deportes en la escuela.
_____

1. ¿Practicas los deportes los fines de semana?

_____

2. ¿Estudias mucho en la casa?

_____

3. ¿Estudias con un amigo o con una amiga?

_____

4. ¿Usas una computadora? ¿Dónde?

_____

5. ¿Cantas muy bien o cantas muy mal?

_____

6. ¿Cantas con un amigo o con una amiga?

_____

7. ¿Pintas en la escuela?

_____

8. ¿Pintas los fines de semana?

_____

¿Cómo lo dices?   Nombre _____

¡APRENDE **MÁS!**   Using a dictionary or glossary is helpful when you can't figure out the meaning of a word. However, many times you can guess the meaning.

Some words in Spanish are similar to words in English. These words are called **cognates**. Usually, cognates are words that come from the same language. For example, many words in Spanish and English come from Latin, which was spoken by the ancient Romans. Look at the examples below.

Latin	English	Spanish
musica	music	música
studere	study	estudiar

You can often guess the meanings of cognates from the way they are spelled or the way they sound. Read the sentences below and circle the words that are cognates of words in English. Then write the English words on the blanks.

1. El   oso   polar   es   blanco   y   grande.

_____

2. La   violeta   es   una   flor   morada.

_____

3. La   computadora   pequeña   es   moderna.

_____

4. La   clase   de   historia   es   interesante.

_____

UNIDAD 4

Nombre _____

La página de diversiones

Un crucigrama

First, read the sentences and fill in the missing words. Then, write the words in the crossword puzzle.

1. Uso _____ computadoras.

2. Voy a pintar _____ mariposas.

3. Hay _____ gatos en la ventana.

4. Uso _____ lápices cuando estudio.

5. Canto el lunes, el martes, el jueves y el sábado.

   Canto _____ días.

6. Dieciséis más _____ son veintidós.

7. Hay dos tigres en mi casa. Hay uno en la ventana y hay _____ en el escritorio.

8. Voy a estudiar _____ libros.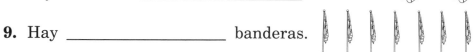

9. Hay _____ banderas.

10. Hay _____ peces.

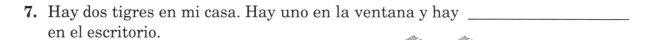

¡Hablemos!   Nombre _____

A. What kinds of weather occur in each season? Using colored pencils or crayons, draw a line from the season to the weather that happens in that season. You may draw more than one line from a season to its weather. Look at the list and use the right color for each season.

la primavera = verde	el verano = anaranjado
el invierno = negro	el otoño = rojo

la primavera

el invierno

el verano

el otoño

¡Hablemos!   Nombre _____

B. When the seasons change, the weather can be different each day of the
week! Use the calendar to answer the question.

lunes	martes	miércoles	jueves	viernes	sábado	domingo
Está nublado.	Hace sol.	Llueve.	Hace viento.	Nieva.	Hace calor.	Hace frío.

M   ¿Qué tiempo hace el domingo?

Hace frío.
_____

1. ¿Qué tiempo hace el miércoles?

_____

4. ¿Qué tiempo hace el viernes?

_____

2. ¿Qué tiempo hace el sábado?

_____

5. ¿Qué tiempo hace el martes?

_____

3. ¿Qué tiempo hace el lunes?

_____

6. ¿Qué tiempo hace el jueves?

_____

¡Hablemos!   Nombre _____

C. Put your thoughts into writing! Look at the lines you drew for exercise A.
Answer each question below by naming the kinds of weather you
connected to the season.

M ¿Qué tiempo hace en el verano?

En el verano hace sol y hace calor.

1. ¿Qué tiempo hace en el otoño?

_____

_____

2. ¿Qué tiempo hace en el invierno?

_____

_____

3. ¿Qué tiempo hace en la primavera?

_____

_____

4. ¿Qué tiempo hace en el verano?

_____

_____

UNIDAD 5

D. Some people like warm, sunny days. Other people like windy, rainy days. What do you think of as good weather and bad weather? Under the column **Buen tiempo**, write the kinds of weather you like. Under the column **Mal tiempo**, write the kinds of weather you do not like.

Buen tiempo	Mal tiempo
_____	_____
_____	_____
_____	_____
_____	_____

Hace frío.   Hace calor.   Nieva.
Hace sol.   Hace viento.   Está nublado.
Llueve.   Hace fresco.

UNIDAD 5

A. Marisol is an exchange student who has come to stay with you. She wants to know what you and your friends like or dislike. To complete the answer to each of her questions, look at the face.

M   ¿A Juan le gusta ir al cine?

Sí, le gusta _____
ir al cine.

3. ¿A Paco le gusta cantar?

_____
cantar.

M   ¿Te gusta cantar?

No, no me gusta _____
cantar.

4. ¿Te gusta ir a la escuela?

_____
ir a la escuela.

1. ¿A Celia le gusta estudiar?

_____
estudiar.

5. ¿A Rosa le gusta ir al cine?

_____
ir al cine.

2. ¿Te gusta pintar?

_____
pintar.

6. ¿Te gusta usar la computadora?

_____
usar la computadora.

¿Cómo lo dices?   Nombre _____

B.   The class newspaper must be ready by tomorrow, but you haven't interviewed Alberto Suárez, the student of the week! Complete the question you ask. Then complete Alberto's answer.

[M]   P: ¿ __**Te gusta**_____ el verano?

　　　R: Sí, __**me gusta**_____ mucho el verano.

1.   P: ¿ _____ la clase de arte?

　　　R: No pinto bien. No _____ la clase de arte.

2.   P: ¿ _____ el gimnasio?

　　　R: Es muy grande. Sí, _____ mucho.

3.   P: ¿ _____ ir a la biblioteca?

　　　R: No estudio mucho. No _____ ir a la biblioteca.

4.   P: ¿ _____ la clase de música?

　　　R: Sí, canto mucho. _____ la clase de música.

¿Cómo lo dices?   Nombre _____

C. You finished your interview with Alberto Suárez. Now it's time to write the story for the newspaper. Read the answers to exercise B before you complete the story for the newspaper.

El alumno de la semana:

Alberto Suárez

El alumno de la semana se llama Alberto Suárez. Es alumno de la escuela

Bolívar. La estación favorita de Alberto es el verano. A Alberto

le gusta mucho el verano
_____ . Alberto no pinta bien. No

_____ .

El gimnasio es muy grande. Alberto practica los deportes en el gimnasio. A

Alberto _____ .

Alberto no estudia mucho. No _____ .

Pero sí _____ . Canta mucho.

¿Cómo lo dices? Nombre _____

D. Imagine that you have been chosen student of the week. What would a story about you be like? Luckily, you can write your own story. Write eight sentences. Write four using **me gusta** and four using **no me gusta**. Then draw a picture.

El alumno de la semana:

_____

(tu nombre)

_____

_____

_____

_____

_____

_____

_____

¿Cómo lo dices?   Nombre _____

E. You're preparing for a test. Which school supplies do you prefer? Use the picture to answer the question.

M   ¿Te gusta la regla larga o la regla corta?

Me gusta la larga. [Me gusta la corta.]

1. ¿Te gusta el lápiz largo o el lápiz corto?

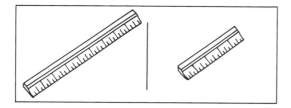

_____

3. ¿Te gusta la computadora grande o la computadora pequeña?

_____

2. ¿Te gusta el cuaderno grande o el cua derno pequeño?

_____

4. ¿Te gusta el bolígrafo negro o el bolígrafo blanco?

_____

¿Cómo lo dices?   Nombre _____

F. You and Ana are walking around the zoo. All the animals seem to be in pairs today. What questions do you ask Ana? Write a question for each sentence.

M   Hay un pájaro azul y un pájaro amarillo.

¿Cuál te gusta, el azul o el amarillo?
_____

1. Hay un gato gris y un gato negro.

_____

2. Hay una mariposa anaranjada y una mariposa roja.

_____

3. Hay un oso marrón y un oso negro.

_____

4. Hay un tigre grande y un tigre pequeño.

_____

5. Hay un pez amarillo y un pez morado.

_____

THINK FAST! ∿∿∿∿∿∿∿∿∿∿∿∿∿∿

Use the picture to answer this question: **¿Qué tiempo hace?**

_____ _____ _____ _____

¿Cómo lo dices?   Nombre _____

¡APRENDE **MÁS!**

Word lists and dictionaries give you more information about words than just a definition. Sometimes that information is abbreviated. Look at the following abbreviations in English. (These are the same abbreviations that appear on page 231 of your textbook.)

adj.	adjective		*inf.*	infinitive
adv.	adverb		*m.*	masculine
com.	command		*pl.*	plural
f.	feminine		*s.*	singular

Use the Spanish – English Word List in your textbook to answer the following questions:

1. Is the word **¡Hablemos!** an adjective, an adverb, or a command? _____

2. On what page do you find the entry for **¡Hablemos!**? _____

3. How many abbreviations follow the word **¡Hablemos!**? _____

4. What are the abbreviations after **¡Hablemos!**? _____

5. On page 237, find the adverb (*adv.*). _____

6. What does the adverb on page 237 mean? _____

7. What are the abbreviations after the entry **¡Practiquemos!**? _____

8. In an exercise titled **¡Practiquemos!**, what do you do? _____

9. What abbreviation follows the word **marrón**? _____

10. What word do you use to mean many things are **marrón**? _____

Nombre _____

La Página de diversiones

Busca las palabras

Read each sentence. Look in the puzzle for the word or words in heavy black letters. Each word may appear across or down in the puzzle. When you find the word, circle it. One has been done for you.

1. **Voy** a la escuela en el **otoño**.

2. **Llueve** en la **primavera**.

3. ¿Qué **tiempo** hace en el **invierno**?

4. Hace **viento** y **hace** much **frío**.

5. Hace **sol** en el **verano**?

6. ¿Está **nevando hoy**?

7. Hace **calor** en el verano.

```
O  T  O  Ñ  O  S  H  B  T  P
N  U  V  I  E  N  T  O  O  R
E  R  B  S  C  C  H  I  V  I
V  L  E  F  H  A  C  E  E  M
A  L  S  R  O  L  V  O  R  A
N  U  O  Í  P  O  O  R  A  V
D  E  H  O  Y  R  Y  T  N  E
O  V  Y  T  I  E  M  P  O  R
Ñ  E  C  X  V  S  O  L  Ñ  A
I  N  V  I  E  R  N  O  Y  T
```

¡Hablemos!   Nombre _____

A.   Marcos is proud of himself! He has spelled all the months of the year correctly! Now he wants you to put the months in the correct order. Marcos has already done the first one.

marzo	agosto	febrero	octubre
noviembre	mayo	julio	abril
✓ enero	septiembre	diciembre	junio

1. __enero__   5. _____   9. _____

2. _____   6. _____   10. _____

3. _____   7. _____   11. _____

4. _____   8. _____   12. _____

B.   Now Marcos wants to write about what he likes and doesn't like to do during certain months. Unfortunately, he scrambled all the letters. Unscramble the letters to form a word. Write it in the blank to complete the sentence for Marcos.

M   Me gusta ____**pintar**____ en abril.
          ratnip

1. Me gusta _____ en junio.
          minarca

2. No me gusta _____ en octubre.
          rabail

3. Me gusta _____ en enero.
          artinpa

4. No me gusta _____ en marzo.
          darna

¡Hablemos!   Nombre _____

C. Susana is showing you pictures of her friends. What is the date? What is each friend doing? Complete the first sentence by writing the appropriate month. Then complete the second sentence by writing an activity.

M

Es el diecisiete de _____**marzo**_____ .

Adela _____**estudia**_____ .

1.

Es el veinte de _____ .

Alberto _____ .

3.

Es el once de _____ .

Marisol _____ .

2.

Es el cinco de _____ .

Lidia _____ .

4.

Es el catorce de _____ .

Daniel _____ .

UNIDAD 6

D. Señor Amable wants to be sure that his park has something for everyone! First, he must find out what people like to do and when they like to do it. How will you fill out his questionnaire? Answer the questions.

¡Un parque para todos!

M ¿Te gusta practicar los deportes?

Sí, me gusta practicar los deportes.

M ¿Cuándo practicas los deportes?

Practico los deportes en julio y agosto.

1. ¿Te gusta patinar?

_____

2. ¿Cuándo patinas?

_____

3. ¿Te gusta nadar?

_____

4. ¿Cuándo nadas?

_____

5. ¿Te gusta caminar?

_____

6. ¿Cuándo caminas?

_____

¿Cómo lo dices?   Nombre _____

A. At the Escuela Buenavista, both students and teachers like to keep busy. Who likes to do each activity? It's hard to tell unless you ask. For each picture, complete the answer by writing **yo, tú, él, ella,** or **usted**.

M   ¿Quién patina?

Él
_____
patina.

3.   ¿Quién camina?

_____
camina.

1.    ¿Quién baila?

_____
bailo.

4.   ¿Quién canta?

_____
canta.

2.    ¿Quién nada?

_____
nadas.

5.   ¿Quién estudia?

_____
estudia.

THINK FAST! ∿∿∿∿∿∿∿∿∿∿∿∿∿∿∿∿∿∿∿

Fill in the missing letters in the sentence. Then write the letters in the blanks below by matching the numbers. You will discover the name of an ancient Mexican civilization that had its own calendar.

Me gu ___ t ___ much ___ bai ___ ar en m ___ r ___ o,
     1   2   3   4   5   6

___ ep ___ iembre y o ___ tubr ___ .
7   8   9   10

___ ___ ___ ___ ___ ___ ___ ___ ___ ___
4 3 7 2 6 8 10 9 5 1

UNIDAD 6

¿Cómo lo dices?   Nombre _____

B. Eduardo is introducing you to people at his school. What questions can you ask about them? Next to each name, write a question about the person.

Paula   Carlos   Luisa   José   Sra. Llanos   Elisa

M (Luisa)   ¿Ella baila muy bien? _____

1. (Elisa) _____

2. (Carlos) _____

3. (Sra. Llanos) _____

4. (Paula) _____

5. (José) _____

C. How does Eduardo answer your questions? Use the pictures and questions in exercise B.

M Paula

Sí, ella patina muy bien. _____

1. Carlos _____

2. Elisa _____

3. Sra. Llanos _____

¿Cómo lo dices?   Nombre _____

D. Choose a partner. Then find out what your partner does at home. You must make up your questions in advance. Then record your partner's answers.

[M] 1. **¿Usas tú la computadora en casa?**
_____

TÚ: ¿Usas tú la computadora en casa?

ALUMNA: Sí yo uso la computadora los fines de semana.

1. **Ella usa la computadora los fines de semana.**
_____

Preguntas

1. _____

2. _____

3. _____

4. _____

5. _____

Respuestas

1. _____

2. _____

3 _____

4. _____

5. _____

¿Cómo lo dices? Nombre _____

E. The Payasos are an unusual couple. Señor Payaso is sensible and a little dull. Señora Payaso is wild and sometimes quite silly. You are a reporter who is interviewing the Payasos. Complete each question and record their answer.

M P: Señor Payaso, ¿quién patina en la casa,

usted o **ella** ?

M R: **Ella patina en la casa. Yo no patino.**

P: Señora Payaso, ¿quién canta en la biblioteca,

usted o **él** ?

R: **Él no canta. Yo canto en la biblioteca.**

1. P: Señor Payaso, ¿quién usa la computadora,

_____ o _____ ?

R: _____

_____

2. P: Señora Payaso, ¿quién nada en enero,

_____ o _____ ?

R: _____

_____

3. P: Señor Payaso, ¿quién baila cn la mesa,

_____ o _____ ?

R: _____

_____

¿Cómo lo dices?   Nombre _____

F. To help you with your reporting job, Francisco showed you part of his schedule for the month. Complete the sentences about his activities with **siempre**, **a veces**, or **nunca**.

L	M	M	J	V	S	D
a d	a b	a b	a b	a c	b	
a d	a	a	a d	a c	b	d
a	a	a b	a b	a	b	

a = ir a la escuela
b = practicar los deportes
c = cantar en la clase de música
d = usar la computadora

M   **Siempre** _____ va a la escuela los miércoles.

1. _____ practica los deportes los miércoles.

2. _____ canta en la clase de música los domingos.

3. _____ usas la computadora los martes.

4. _____ practica los deportes los sábados.

G. What do you like to do in your spare time? Complete the questions in this survey by using **siempre**, **a veces**, or **nunca**. Fill out the survey by writing your own answers.

M ¿ **Siempre** _____ estudias en casa?

Sí, siempre estudio en casa _____ .

1. ¿ _____ patinas en el invierno?

_____ .

2. ¿Bailas _____ en febrero?

_____ .

3. ¿ _____ usas la computadora en agosto?

_____ .

4. ¿ _____ nadas en diciembre?

_____ .

5. ¿ _____ vas a la escuela en julio?

_____ .

¿Cómo lo dices?   Nombre _____

The names of the months in most of Europe and America all come from the calendar created in ancient Rome—the Julian calendar. The Julian calendar was not perfect, and so it was revised in the sixteenth century. The new, improved calendar was called the Gregorian calendar. Although the calendar was improved, the names of the months stayed the same.

The lists below are in five different languages: English, French, German, Italian, and Spanish. Study the lists and guess which language each list is in. Write the letter of the list on the blank beside the name of the language. (Two of them should be very easy for you!)

a	b	c	d	e
janvier	Januar	enero	gennaio	January
février	Februar	febrero	febbraio	February
mars	März	marzo	marzo	March
avril	April	abril	aprile	April
mai	Mai	mayo	maggio	May
juin	Juni	junio	giugno	June
juillet	Juli	julio	luglio	July
août	August	agosto	agosto	August
septembre	September	septiembre	settembre	September
octobre	Oktober	octubre	ottobre	October
novembre	November	noviembre	nobembre	November
décembre	Dezember	diciembre	dicembre	December

_____ English   _____ German   _____ Spanish

_____ French   _____ Italian

Nombre _____

La Página de diversiones

Una frase feliz

Complete each sentence with a word from the box. Then use the numbers to discover the secret phrase.

√ año	octubre	nadar	patinar
gusta	voy	enero	agosto

1. Doce meses son un __a__ __ñ__ __o__ .
   <u>1</u>   <u>2</u>   <u>3</u>

2. Me gusta ____ ____ ____ ____ ____ en el verano.
      4   5   6   7   8

3. Llueve y hace viento en ____ ____ ____ ____ ____ ____ ____ .
      9   10   11   12   13   14   15

4. En ____ ____ ____ ____ ____ nieva y hace frío.
     16   17   18   19   20

5. En ____ ____ ____ ____ ____ ____ hace sol y hace calor.
     21   22   23   24   25   26

6. No ____ ____ ____ a la escuela en el verano.
     27   28   29

7. A María le gusta ____ ____ ____ ____ ____ ____ ____ en febrero.
      30   31   32   33   34   35   36

8. A Natán le ____ ____ ____ ____ ____ bailar siempre.
     37   38   39   40   41

What do you say on New Year's Day?

¡P __ __´ __ __ __ __ __ __ñ__ __ __ __ __ __ __ !
  8   23   39   30   16   36   3   7   2   28   17   38   15   27   9

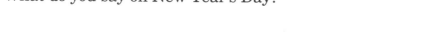

Unidades 4–6   Nombre _____

A. The students in señora Lozano's class are daydreaming while they wait for the cafeteria line to move. Complete each sentence according to the picture.

M A Zoraida **le gusta el verano.** _____

1. A Alberto **le gusta cantar (*or* la clase de música).** _____

2. A Rosita _____

3. A Juan _____

4. A Ramón _____

5. A Arsenio _____

_____

¿Cómo lo dices?   Nombre _____

B. You are participating in a survey of student likes and dislikes. Choose the answer that comes closest to how you feel. Then write the complete sentence on the lines below.

[M] Me gusta...

   a. estudiar

   b. pintar

   (c.) cantar

1. Me gusta mucho...

   a. el invierno

   b. el otoño

   c. la primavera

   d. el verano

2. No me gusta...

   a. practicar los deportes

   b. cantar

   c. estudiar

   d. pintar

3. Me gusta...

   a. ir al cine

   b. ir a la biblioteca

   c. ir a la escuela

   d. ir al gimnasio

4. No me gusta...

   a. la clase de arte

   b. la clase de música

   c. el gimnasio

   d. la clase de computadoras

[M] **Me gusta cantar.**
_____

1. _____

2. _____

3. _____

4. _____

Unidades 4–6   Nombre _____

C. At summer camp, Elena Bosque is planning activities. First, she needs to know what people do. To complete each answer, underline the correct word.

M ¿Quién camina mucho, tú o Alfredo?
(Yo, <u>Él</u>) camina mucho.

1. ¿Quién nada muy bien, el señor Guzmán o tú?
(Yo, Él) nado muy bien.

2. Señora Elías, ¿quién pinta muy bien, usted o Alicia?
(Yo, Ella) pinta muy bien.

3. Enrique, ¿quién camina mucho, tú o yo?
(Yo, Tú) caminas mucho.

4. ¿Quién canta muy bien, tú o Federico?
(Yo, Él) canta muy bien.

D. Now Elena wants to know what you do. What are her questions? Write them on the blanks.

M ¿ / practicar / los deportes / ?

¿Practicas los deportes? _____

1. ¿ / caminar / mucho / ?   **3.** ¿ / cantar / muy / bien / ?

_____   _____

2. ¿ / pintar / muy / bien / ?   **4.** ¿ / bailar / mucho / ?

_____   _____

¿Cómo lo dices?　　　Nombre _____

E. You are very curious about Rita's after-school activities. How does Rita answer your questions? Use the calendar to answer the questions.

lunes	martes	miércoles	jueves	viernes
la clase de trompeta	la casa de Ana	el gimnasio	la clase de trompeta	el cine
y	y	y	y	y
estudiar	bailar	practicar los deportes	estudiar	caminar— la casa de Luis

[M] ¿Adónde vas el jueves?

Voy a la clase de trompeta.

[M] ¿Qué vas a hacer el lunes?

Voy a estudiar.

1. ¿Adónde vas el viernes?

_____

2. ¿Qué vas a hacer el miércoles?

_____

3. ¿Adónde vas el martes?

_____

4. ¿Qué vas a hacer el jueves?

_____

5. ¿Adónde vas el miércoles?

_____

6. ¿Qué vas a hacer el viernes?

_____

Unidades 4–6   Nombre _____

F. Little Paquito is curious about Rita's activities, too. How do you answer Paquito's questions? Use the calendar on page 96 to check Rita's schedule and write your answers.

M ¿Qué hace Rita el jueves?

Va a la clase de trompeta y estudia.

1. ¿Qué hace Rita el viernes?

_____

2. ¿Qué hace Rita el lunes?

_____

3. ¿Qué hace Rita el miércoles?

_____

4. ¿Qué hace Rita el martes?

_____

THINK FAST!

The pet shop is about to close. Make a decision about which animal you like better.

¿Cuál te gusta, la tortuga grande o la tortuga pequeña?

_____

¿Cuál te gusta, el lagarto largo o el lagarto corto?

_____

Nombre _____

G. How well do you know yourself? How well do you know your classmate? Take the following quiz. First answer according to what you like. Then answer according to what you think your classmate likes. Compare answers with your classmate to find out if you were right.

M   ¿Cuál bolígrafo te gusta?

Me gusta el largo. Le gusta
_____

el corto. [Le gusta el largo.]
_____

1. ¿Cuál gato te gusta?

_____

_____

_____

3. ¿Cuál mariposa te gusta?

_____

_____

_____

2. ¿Cuál casa te gusta?

_____

_____

_____

4. ¿Cuál loro te gusta?

_____

_____

_____

¡Hablemos!   Nombre _____

A. Try this guessing game. What do the pictures remind you of? Answer the question **¿Qué tienes?**

M

Tengo sed.
_____

1.
_____

2.
_____

3.
_____

4.
_____

5.
_____

B. Many people in your neighborhood have birthdays this month. How do they answer the question **¿Cuántos años tienes?**

M Adela / 15   **Tengo quince años.**
_____

1. Fernando / 6   _____

2. Luisa / 22   _____

3. Rosita / 3   _____

4. Manuel / 13   _____

¡Hablemos! Nombre _____

C. Ignacio is having a hard day. Describe Ignacio's day. Match each sentence to the correct picture. (Be careful! There are more pictures than sentences.)

No tiene razón.

Tiene prisa.

No tiene suerte.

Tiene dolor.

Tiene miedo.

Tiene hambre.

Tiene frío.

UNIDAD 7

¿Cómo lo dices?   Nombre _____

A. You are about to meet Samuel's family. What pronoun will you use with each person, **tú** or **usted**? Underline your answer.

M

tú   usted

1.

tú   usted

2.

tú   usted

3.

tú   usted

4.

tú   usted

5.

tú   usted

B. It's Talent Night at the community center. What a talented group of people! Use the word in parentheses to complete the sentence saying what each person does well.

Señorita Vásquez, **usted canta** _____ muy bien. (cantar)

1. Martín, _____ muy bien. (bailar)

2. Josefina, _____ muy bien. (pintar)

3. Señor Suárez, _____ muy bien. (cantar)

4. Señora Calvo, _____ muy bien. (patinar)

5. Vicente, _____ los deportes muy bien. (practicar)

6. Señorita Martínez, _____ muy bien. (nadar)

¿Cómo lo dices?　　　Nombre _____

C. Beatriz has interviewed many people at her school. You have found her notes. What questions did she ask? Write them on the blanks.

M　La señora Trillo patina mucho.

　　¿Patina usted mucho? _____

1. Estela camina mucho los sábados.

　　_____　_____

2. Ricardo usa la computadora en la biblioteca.

　　_____

3. El señor Perales nada todos los días.

　　_____

4. La señorita Ojeda va al gimnasio los viernes.

　　_____

5. Gilberto no practica los deportes.

　　_____

THINK FAST! ∿∿∿∿∿∿∿∿∿∿∿∿∿∿∿∿

What would you say if you found a pot of gold? Follow the arrows and write the words in the blanks.

¡ ___ ___ ___ ___ ___ ___

___ ___ ___ ___ ___ ___

___ ___ ___ ___ ___ ___ ___ !

UNIDAD 7

¿Cómo lo dices?   Nombre _____

D. Señor Montalvo's class held a rummage sale. What did everyone buy?
Complete and answer the question according to the picture. Use **tengo,
tienes,** or **tiene**.

M   P: ¿Qué _____**tiene**_____ Alberto?

     R: Él _____**tiene**_____ un oso negro.

1. P: Señor Montalvo, ¿qué _____ usted?

     R: _____ un globo grande.

2. P: Elisa, ¿qué _____ tú?

     R: _____ un loro.

3. P: ¿Qué _____ Verónica?

     R: Ella _____ un calendario.

4. P: Daniel, ¿qué _____ tú?

     R: _____ un mapa.

5. P: Señora Vega, ¿qué _____ usted?

     R: _____ unos peces.

6. P: ¿Qué _____ Rafael?

     R: Él _____ unos libros.

¿Cómo lo dices?   Nombre _____

E.   What would you ask a friend in each situation? Use **tener** and the word in parentheses to write a question.

M   No estoy bien. Estoy muy mal.

(la gripe)   **¿Tienes la gripe?** _____

1. Es enero. Hace viento y está nevando.

(frío)   _____

2. Es julio. Hace mucho sol.

(calor)   _____

3. Es una noche oscura. Camino a la casa.

(miedo)   _____

4. Estoy mal. No voy a la escuela.

(dolor)   _____

F.   How would you answer the questions you wrote in exercise E? You are answering for your friend and for yourself.

M   **Mi amigo (Mi amiga) tiene la gripe. Tengo la gripe.**

1. _____

2. _____

3. _____

4. _____

Nombre _____

▦▦▦ EXPRESA TUS IDEAS ▱▱▷

The Explorers' Club visited the Tropical World exhibit at the zoo. Señorita Aventura took a picture of the members. It's your job to write a story for the club newspaper. Write at least five sentences about the picture.

hay	calor	hambre	grande
hace	dolor	sueño	muchachos
tener	sed	miedo	muchachas

_____

_____

_____

_____

_____

_____

_____

_____

Nombre _____

La página de diversiones

Una nota secreta

Patricia has passed you a note in class. Break the secret code to find out what she is saying. Circle the letters in the note to form words. Then write each letter in order.

(T) I J K E I J K N I J K

G I J K O I J K M I J K

U I J K C I J K H I J K

A I J K H I J K A I J K

M I J K B I J K R I J K

E I J K

¡ __T__ __ __ __ __ __ __ __ __ __

__ __ __ __ __ __ __ __ __ __

__ __ __ __ __ __ __ __ !

¡Hablemos!   Nombre _____

A. Margarita is impatient. Fifteen minutes seem like an hour to her. Color the clocks to show her when you will do different activities.

M Voy a la escuela en media hora.

1. Voy a estudiar en dos horas.

2. Voy a bailar en un cuarto de hora.

3. Voy a usar la computadora en una hora.

4. Voy a la casa en media hora.

5. Voy a caminar en una hora y cuarto.
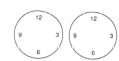

6. Voy al gimnasio en una hora y media.
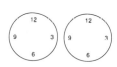

UNIDAD 8

¡Hablemos!   Nombre _____

B. You are having lunch in the school's cafeteria. While you are eating, you hear several conversations. Complete the sentences by using **por la mañana, por la tarde,** or **por la noche**.

M —¿Cuándo vas a la biblioteca, Martín?

—Voy los sábados ___por la mañana___ .

1. —Y tú, María, ¿cuándo vas al cine?

—Voy el miércoles _____ .

2. —Jesús, ¿cuándo vas a la tienda?

—Voy los domingos _____ .

3. —Elisa patina los lunes por la noche.

—No, ella patinas los jueves _____ .

C. How observant are you? Look at the pictures and decide at what time of day the activities take place. Write a sentence telling what you decided.

el mediodía   la salida del sol   la medianoche   la puesta del sol

M

1.

2.

_____   _____   _____

_____   _____   _____

3.

4.

5.

_____   _____   _____

_____   _____   _____

UNIDAD 8

A. Hortensia has made a chart to teach her brother how to tell time. Help her finish the chart. Draw a line from the sentence to the right clock. (Careful! There are too many clocks!)

M   Son las ocho en punto.

1. Son las cuatro y cinco.

2. Es la una en punto.

3. Son las siete y cuarto.

4. Son las tres y media.

UNIDAD 8

¿Cómo lo dices?   Nombre _____

B. You should have changed the battery in your watch. It's running five minutes slow. Tell the right time by adding five minutes to the time on the clock. Write a sentence.

M     Son las tres _____

y cinco. _____

1.    _____
_____
_____

2.    _____
_____
_____

3.    _____
_____
_____

4.    _____
_____
_____

5.    _____
_____
_____

THINK FAST! ∿∿∿∿∿∿∿∿∿∿∿∿∿∿∿∿

Ricky wants you to go to the movies with him. Decode his message by unscrambling the letters and writing the words on the lines.

¿A _____ _____ _____ al _____ ?
　　éuq　　　aohr　　　avs　　　　enic

Voy a _____ _____ _____ _____ .
　　　lsa　　　occni　　　ne　　　unpto

UNIDAD 8

¿Cómo lo dices? Nombre _____

---

c. You are performing a scientific experiment this Saturday from 7:00 A.M. until 11:00 P.M. Every time one of your canaries walks across the cage to ring a bell, you will record the time. Answer the questions according to the clock. Use **de la mañana, de la tarde,** or **de la noche**.

M
8:06

Ahora camina Albertina. ¿Qué hora es?

Son las ocho y seis de la mañana.

1. **9:07**

Ahora camina Robertico. ¿Qué hora es?

_____

2. **11:02**

Ahora camina Julieta. ¿Qué hora es?

_____

3. **1:00**

Ahora camina Albertina. ¿Qué hora es?

_____

4. **6:14**

Ahora camina Julieta. ¿Qué hora es?

_____

5. **10:16**

Ahora camina Robertico. ¿Qué hora es?

_____

¿Cómo lo dices?   Nombre _____

D. Gregorio is telling you about his day. What time does he do different things?
Match the clocks to his statements by writing the number of the clock that
goes with the sentence.

1.   2.   3.   4.   5.

_____3_____ |M| Camino a la escuela a las nueve menos diez.

_____ a. Voy a la clase de arte a las once menos cuarto.

_____ b. Voy al gimnasio a las doce menos veinticinco.

_____ c. Camino a la casa la una menos cinco.

_____ d. Estudio a las tres menos cinco.

E. What questions can you ask Gregorio? Match the following questions with
his statements in exercise A. Write the letter that goes with the question.

_____M_____ |M| ¿A qué hora caminas a la escuela?

_____ 1. ¿Cuándo vas a la clase de arte?

_____ 2. ¿Cuándo caminas a la casa?

_____ 3. ¿A qué hora estudias?

_____ 4. ¿A qué hora vas al gimnasio?

UNIDAD 8

F. You want to keep track of your brothers and sisters' activities. How do they answer your questions? Complete the answer according to the clock.

M P: Felipe, ¿cuándo vas a estudiar?

R: Voy a estudiar _____**a las cuatro menos veinte.**_____

| 3:40 |

1. P: Esperanza, ¿cuándo vas a cantar?

R: Voy a cantar _____

| 4:45 |

2. P: Raimundo, ¿a qué hora vas al cine?

R: Voy al cine _____

| 7:50 |

3. P: Carmen, ¿a qué hora vas a la biblioteca?

R: Voy a la biblioteca _____

| 11:35 |

4. P: María, ¿cuándo usas la computadora?

R: Uso la computadora _____

| 12:51 |

5. P: Víctor, ¿a qué hora caminas al gimnasio?

R: Camino al gimnasio _____

| 9:40 |

G. Bárbara and Berta are best friends. On Saturday, they like to spend a lot of time together. They even made a schedule of their activities. Answer the question according to the schedule.

Bárbara	**Berta**
8:40 / la clase de arte	9:30 / la casa
9:38 / la casa de Berta	11:00 / la casa de Bárbara
11:00 / la casa	1:20 / la clase de computadoras
3:40 / la biblioteca	3:35 / la biblioteca

M ¿A qué hora va Bárbara a la clase de arte?

Va a la clase de arte a las nueve menos veinte.

_____

1. ¿Cuándo va Berta a la casa de Bárbara?

_____

2. ¿Cuándo va Bárbara a la casa de Berta?

_____

3. ¿A qué hora va Berta a la clase de computadoras?

_____

4. ¿A qué hora va Berta a la biblioteca?

_____

5. ¿Cuándo camina Bárbara a la biblioteca?

_____

¿Cómo lo dices?   Nombre _____

H.   You dropped your note cards and got them all mixed up. Match the
         questions with the answers by writing the letter of the correct answer next
         to the question.

1. ¿Cómo te llamas?   _____d_____   a.   Es Mariano Huerta.

2. ¿Adónde vas?   _____   b.   Bailo a las seis y cuarto.

3. ¿Qué día es hoy?   _____   c.   Hay cinco lápices.

4. ¿Qué es esto?   _____   d.   Me llamo Ana Gómez.

5. ¿Quién es?   _____   e.   Voy al cine.

6. ¿Qué hora es?   _____   f.   Es una pizarra.

7. ¿A qué hora bailas? _____   g.   Son las seis y cuarto.

8. ¿Cuántos lápices hay? _____   h.   Es miércoles.

THINK FAST! ∿∿∿∿∿∿∿∿∿∿∿∿∿∿

As fast as you can, answer the following questions:

1. ¿Cuál es tu número de teléfono?

_____

2. ¿Cuántos años tienes tú?

_____

¿Cómo lo dices?   Nombre _____

I. You are interviewing a foreign exchange student. Complete your question with the correct question word.

Cuál   Adónde   Quién   Dónde
Cuándo   Cómo   Qué   A qué hora

M   RITA: ¿ **Dónde** _____ estudias los lunes?
    ÓSCAR: Estudio en la biblioteca.

1. RITA: ¿ _____ vas a la casa por la tarde?
    ÓSCAR: Voy a la casa a las cuatro menos veinte.

2. RITA: ¿ _____ haces los sábados por la noche?
    ÓSCAR: A veces voy al cine los sábados.

3. RITA: ¿ _____ es tu animal favorito?
    ÓSCAR: Mi animal favorito es el elefante.

4. RITA: ¿ _____ son los elefantes?
    ÓSCAR: Son del color gris. Son muy grandes.

J. Write three statements about yourself. Then write three questions you would ask a friend to find out the same information.

Statements	Questions
M Tengo muchos amigos.	M ¿Cuántos amigos tienes?
1. _____	1. _____
2. _____	2. _____
3. _____	3. _____

¿Cómo lo dices?   Nombre _____

In Spanish, as in English, there are more ways than one to state the time. Often Spanish-speaking people use the verb **faltar**, which means "to be lacking," to state the time before the hour. Occasionally, you will hear Spanish-speaking people who have lived in the United States adapt their language to the English form. Look at the clock below and read three ways you may hear people answer the question: **¿Qué hora es?**

1. Son las cinco menos veinticinco.
2. Faltan veinticinco minutos para las cinco.
3. Son las cuatro y treinta y cinco.

The first sentence follows the way you are learning. Spanish-speaking people all over the world will understand you if you use this pattern.

The second sentence uses the verb **faltar**. It is a way of saying "It's twenty-five to five."

The third sentence uses Spanish words with the English way of telling time. It's the same as saying, "It's four thirty-five."

Read the following examples. Then write the same time in the way you have learned.

1. Faltan veinte minutos para las diez.

2. Son las nueve y cuarenta.

3. _____

1. Faltan quince minutos para la una.

2. Son las doce y cuarenta y cinco.

3. _____

Nombre _____

La página de diversiones

¿Quién tiene la pelota?

Detective Carlota Curiosa has been called to the Colegio Juárez to find out who took a soccer ball from the gymnasium. All she knows is that the ball (**la pelota**) was there on Tuesday at 1:00 P.M., but it was missing at 2:00 P.M. As a detective in training, you must read the testimony from the suspects and form your own conclusion!

Mario del Barrio

P: ¿A qué hora vas al gimnasio?
R: Siempre voy al gimnasio a las dos en punto. Tengo una clase a las dos.

Señor Olvida

P: ¿Cuándo va usted al gimnasio?
R: Voy al gimnasio a las dos menos veinte. Busco un globo. Mario practica los deportes con mis globos.

Susana Banda

P: ¿Qué haces a la una de la tarde?
R: Siempre voy a la clase de música a la una en punto. Voy al gimnasio a las nueve de la mañana.

Señora Rústica

P: ¿Cuándo va usted al gimnasio?
R: A veces voy al gimnasio a la una menos cuarto. Me gusta practicar los deportes. Los martes voy a la biblioteca.

¿Quién tiene la pelota?

_____ tiene la pelota.

Mira la página 120 para la solución.

¡Hablemos!   Nombre _____

A. You are comparing schedules with Marta. How does she answer your questions? Complete the answer according to the picture.

M ¿Adónde vas a las ocho de la mañana?

Voy a la clase de _____**ciencias.**_____

1. ¿Adónde vas a las nueve menos diez?

Voy a la clase de _____

2. ¿Adónde vas a las diez menos veinte?

Voy a la clase de _____

3. ¿Adónde vas a la una y media de la tarde?

Voy a la clase de _____

4. ¿Adónde vas a las dos y veinte?

Voy a la clase de _____

UNIDAD 9

¡Hablemos!   Nombre _____

B. Gabriela is interviewing her classmates to find out which classes students like best. How do they answer her questions? Use the words in parentheses to write two answers.

[M] P: Raúl, ¿cuál es tu clase favorita? ¿Por qué?

R: (matemáticas / divertido)

Es la clase de matemáticas. Es divertida.

1. P: Juana, ¿cuál es tu clase favorita? ¿Por qué?

R: (historia / fácil)

_____

2. P: Jorge, ¿cuál es tu clase favorita? ¿Por qué?

R: (salud / fantástico)

_____

3. P: María, ¿cuál es tu clase favorita? ¿Por qué?

R: (ciencias / interesante)

_____

4. P: Gilberto, ¿cuál es tu clase favorita? ¿Por qué?

R: (español / importante)

_____

Solución a **¿Quién tiene la pelota?** de la página 118.

El señor Olvida _____ tiene la pelota.

¡Hablemos!   Nombre _____

C.   Now Gabriela is interviewing you. Write your answers.

M   ¿Te gusta la clase de educación física?

No, no me gusta la clase de educación física.

M   ¿Por qué?

La clase es aburrida y muy difícil.

1. ¿Te gusta la clase de ciencias?

_____

2. ¿Por qué?

_____

3. ¿Te gusta la clase de inglés?

_____

4. ¿Por qué?

_____

5. ¿Cuál es tu clase favorita?

_____

6. ¿Por qué?

_____

THINK FAST! ∿∿∿∿∿∿∿∿∿∿∿∿∿

Unscramble the letters to find out what Josefina thinks of one of her classes.

¡La clase de _____ es _____ !
              ihortisa   rrudaabi

_____

UNIDAD 9

¿Cómo lo dices?   Nombre _____

A. You love pets and zoo animals. Underline **gusta** or **gustan** to complete the sentence about all the animals you like.

M   Me (gusta / <u>gustan</u>) los perros.

1. Me (gusta / gustan) el tigre.

2. Me (gusta / gustan) los flamencos.

3. Me (gusta / gustan) el pájaro.

4. Me (gusta / gustan) los osos.

5. Me (gusta / gustan) los loros.

6. Me (gusta / gustan) los canarios.

7. Me (gusta / gustan) las mariposas.

8. Me (gusta / gustan) los conejos.

9. Me (gusta / gustan) el pez.

10. Me (gusta / gustan) el ratón.

B. Francisco wants to play baseball all day. He doesn't like to go to school. Use **gusta** or **gustan** to complete the sentence about the things Francisco doesn't like.

M   No me ___**gustan**___ los libros.

1. No me _____ las clases.

2. No me _____ el inglés.

3. No me _____ las computadoras.

4. No me _____ los pupitres.

5. No me _____ la música.

6. No me _____ el arte.

7. No me _____ las ciencias.

8. No me _____ el español.

9. No me _____ la historia.

10. No me _____ los lápices.

¿Cómo lo dices?   Nombre _____

C. You and Elvira are making T-shirts for your friends. Each shirt will have a picture of something each friend likes or dislikes. Answer Elvira's questions according to the faces.

M ¿A Carlos le gusta el arte?

Sí, le gusta el arte. _____

_____

1. ¿A Javier le gusta el invierno?

_____

_____

2. ¿A Inés le gustan los libros?

_____

_____

3. ¿A Norma le gustan las clases?

_____

_____

4. ¿A Paco le gustan los osos?

_____

_____

5. ¿A Lola le gustan los muchachos?

_____

_____

THINK FAST! ∧∧∧∧∧∧∧∧∧∧∧∧∧∧∧∧∧∧∧

Answer the question below and then draw a design of what you like on the T-shirt.

¿Qué te gusta?

_____

_____

_____

¿Cómo lo dices?   Nombre _____

D. You and Elvira are ready to give your friends the T-shirts. Tell what each person likes or doesn't like. Use the picture and the name to write a sentence.

M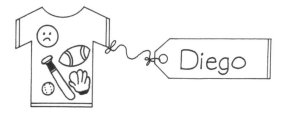

A Diego no le gustan los deportes.
_____

1.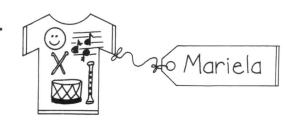
_____
_____

2.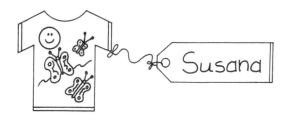
_____
_____

3.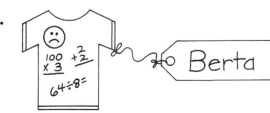
_____
_____

4.
_____
_____

5.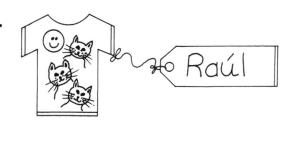
_____
_____

¿Cómo lo dices?   Nombre _____

E.   Estela is taking a survey for social studies class. She wants to find out what activities people like to learn. Study her list and help her write her notes.

[M] (Mateo / la historia)

Mateo   **aprende la historia.** _____

(Franciso / a nadar)

Franciso   **aprende a nadar.** _____

(Margarita / el español)

1. Margarita _____

(Juan / a patinar)

2. Juan _____

(Adela / a nadar)

3. Adela _____

(Luis / las matemáticas)

4. Luis _____

(Manola / a bailar)

5. Luis _____

(Horacio / a usar la computadora)

6. Horacio _____

THINK FAST! 〰〰〰〰〰〰〰〰〰〰

¿Qué aprendes tú?

_____

_____

¿Cómo lo dices?   Nombre _____

F. You have written a letter to your pen pal in Venezuela. Use the appropriate form of the word in parentheses to complete each sentence.

---

11 de enero

¡Hola, Óscar!

¿Cómo estás? Estoy muy bien. (**M**) Yo _____**escribo**_____ (escribir) esta

carta en la casa. (1) Yo _____ (aprender) el español en la escuela.

(2) ¿_____ (aprender) tú el inglés? (3) ¿_____

(escribir) tú en inglés? (4) Yo _____ (leer) mucho en la clase de

inglés. (5) Yo siempre _____ (comprender) las lecciones.

(6) También _____ (pintar) mucho en la clase de arte. (7) Mi amigo

Pepe también _____ (pintar). (8) En mi escuela, _____

(aprender) a usar las computadoras. (9) Y tú, ¿qué _____ (aprender)?

¡Hasta pronto!

_____

(tu nombre)

¿Cómo lo dices?   Nombre _____

G. Señora Martínez has just given a demonstration of how to dance the cha-cha. To make sure that everyone understands, she asks a question. Complete her question. Then use **sí** or **no** to write the answer.

M̄ Señor Luna, ¿ __comprende__ usted la pregunta?

(No) __No, no comprendo la pregunta.__

1. Alicia, ¿ _____ tú la pregunta?

(Sí) _____

2. Rodrigo, ¿ _____ tú la pregunta?

(No) _____

3. Señorita del Valle, ¿ _____ usted la pregunta?

(No) _____

4. Señora Beltrán, ¿ _____ usted la pregunta?

(Sí) _____

H. Now make a list for señora Martínez. Use the answers in exercise G to complete the list.

El señor Luna __no comprende__ .   3. La señorita del Valle _____

1. Alicia _____ .   _____ .

2. Rodrigo _____ .   4. La señora Beltrán _____ .

¿Cómo lo dices?   Nombre _____

I. You have been selected to appear with other "super-brains" on the game show *Los super-cerebros*. Each contestant is given a situation and uses the clues to state what the subject does in that situation. Write the statements in your own words. Good luck!

M La profesora escribe una pregunta en la pizarra.
(El alumno / leer)

El alumno lee la pregunta.

1. Un compañero de clase tiene un número de teléfono. Tú tienes un cuaderno y un lápiz. (Yo / escribir)

_____

2. Hace mucho frío. A Juanita le gusta practicar deportes. (Ella / patinar)

_____

3. Enrique va a la biblioteca. Hay un libro interesante. (Él / leer)

_____

4. La señora Molina lee libros en inglés. Ella escribe mucho en inglés. (Ella / comprender)

_____

5. Tú lees la lección de historia. Escribes todas las respuestas. (Yo / comprender)

_____

6. Diego va a la clase de computadoras. La clase es muy aburrida. Él nunca escribe en el cuaderno. Nunca tiene razón. (Él / aprender)

_____

EXPRESA TUS IDEAS

The Explorers' Club is holding a special meeting at school on Saturday. The members are supposed to plan their summer trip. No one seems to be paying attention! Use the words below to write at least five sentences about the picture.

leer	estudiar	interesante	importante
escribir	aprender	terrible	divertido
gustar	comprender	mucho	fantástico

_____

_____

_____

_____

_____

_____

_____

Nombre _____

La Página de diversiones

Busca la palabra

Read each sentence. Look in the puzzle for the word or words in heavy **black** letters. Each word may appear across or down in the puzzle. When you find a word, circle it. One is done for you.

1. **Escribo con** un **lápiz** en el **cuaderno**.
2. A mí **me gusta** la **clase** de **salud**.
3. ¿A ti te **gustan** las **ciencias**?
4. La **geografía** es **aburrida**.
5. ¡Qué **terrible**! Paco no **comprende** la **lección**.
6. **Siempre aprendo mucho** en las clases.
7. La **pregunta** es **muy fácil**.

```
M  J  C  U  A  D  E  R  N  O  L  Q  R  Ñ
U  X  I  P  R  E  G  U  N  T  A  U  T  C
Y  G  E  O  G  R  A  F  Í  A  U  É  Q  O
M  O  N  X  T  Y  C  L  A  S  E  Z  A  N
E  S  C  R  I  B  O  V  E  N  T  A  N  A
P  A  I  B  G  E  M  U  C  H  O  M  U  L
A  L  A  Ó  R  F  P  L  A  B  R  E  S  E
G  U  S  T  A  T  R  Ñ  P  C  I  C  Ó  C
A  D  I  R  N  T  E  R  R  I  B  L  E  C
L  Á  P  I  Z  E  N  T  E  N  Z  R  Q  I
A  B  U  R  R  I  D  A  N  Á  B  P  R  Ó
S  I  E  M  P  R  E  D  D  B  R  U  R  N
S  O  G  U  S  T  A  N  O  F  Á  C  I  L
```

¡Hablemos!   Nombre _____

A. You love fantasy stories. The book you're reading now is about the president of Andalandia and the members of his family. You have drawn his family tree. Use the picture to complete the sentence.

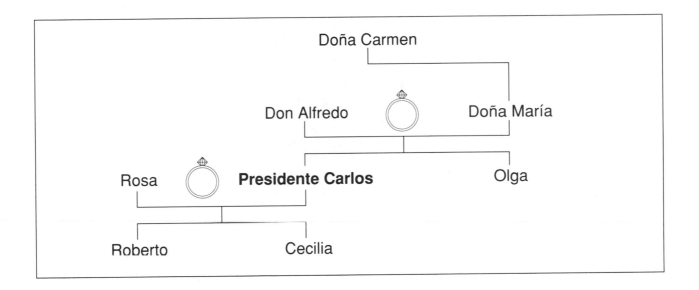

Doña Carmen

Don Alfredo   Doña María

Rosa   **Presidente Carlos**   Olga

Roberto   Cecilia

[M] Doña María es ___**la mamá**___ del presidente.

1. Olga es _____ del presidente.

2. Doña Carmen es _____ del presidente.

3. Roberto es _____ del presidente.

4. Don Alfredo es _____ del presidente.

5. Cecilia es _____ del presidente.

6. Don Alfredo y doña María son _____ del presidente.

¡Hablemos!   Nombre _____

B. Gerardo has written two paragraphs about his family. After reading the paragraphs, answer the questions.

La familia de Gerardo

Me llamo Gerardo Pérez. Tengo una familia grande. Mi papá se llama Humberto. Mi madrastra se llama Antonia. Tengo tres hermanos y dos hermanas. Mi familia es divertida.

Tengo seis tíos y cuatro tías. Tengo diez primos. Mi primo favorito se llama Alejandro. Mi prima favorita se llama Carlota. Mi tío Gerónimo es mi tío favorito. Él es interesante.

M ¿Cuántas tías tiene Gerardo?

Tiene cuatro tías. _____

1. ¿Cuántos tíos tiene Gerardo?

   _____

2. ¿Cómo se llama el papá de Gerardo?

   _____

3. ¿Cómo se llama la madrastra?

   _____

4. ¿Quién es el primo favorito?

   _____

5. ¿Quién es la prima favorita?

   _____

6. ¿Cuántos hermanos y hermanas tiene?

   _____

7. ¿Cómo es la familia de Gerardo?

   _____

8. ¿Cómo es el tío Gerónimo?

   _____

¡Hablemos!　　　　　　Nombre _____

C. What is your family tree like? Draw a family tree and write a paragraph like Gerardo's in exercise B.

_____　___

_____

_____

_____

_____

_____

_____

_____

¿Cómo lo dices?   Nombre _____

A. You have volunteered to work in the Lost and Found booth at the school carnival. What questions do you ask people? How do they answer you? Use **mi, mis, tu, tus, su,** or **sus** to complete each question and answer.

M    ¿Es __su__ perro?

Sí, es __mi__ perro.

M    ¿Son __tus__ mapas?

Sí, son __mis__ mapas.

1.    ¿Es _____ hijo?

Sí, es _____ hijo.

2.    ¿Es _____ papá?

Sí, es _____ papá.

3.    ¿Son _____ loros?

Sí, son _____ loros.

4.    ¿Son _____ libros?

Sí, son _____ libros.

5.    ¿Son _____ hijos?

Sí, son _____ hijos.

6.    ¿Es _____ reloj?

Sí, es _____ reloj.

THINK FAST! ∼∼∼∼∼∼∼∼∼∼∼∼∼∼∼

How quickly can you solve the following puzzlers?

1. El papá de mi abuela es mi _____ .

2. La hermana de mi papá es mi _____ .

3. La hija de mi abuela es mi _____ .

¿Cómo lo dices?   Nombre _____

B.   Natán's relatives visited him on his birthday. He drew a picture of the grand family event and wrote a paragraph. Help him finish it.

(M) ___Mi___ familia es grande. (**1**) _____ abuelo se llama Adán. (**2**) _____

abuela se llama Irene. (**3**) _____ hermanos son León y Andrés. (**4**) Darío y Lucía

son _____ tíos. (**5**) _____ hijos son Rubén y Hugo. (**6**) _____ hijas son Nora

y Ema.

¿Cómo lo dices?   Nombre _____

C. If you're going to be an ace reporter, you'll have to interview lots of people. Find one adult and one person your own age to interview. First, write two questions for each person about his or her family. Then, write the answers.

 M P: __**Señora Ruiz, ¿es grande su familia?**_____

 R: __**No, mi familia no es grande.**_____

Nombre: _____

1. P: _____

 R: _____

2. P: _____

 R: _____

Nombre: _____

1. P: _____

 R: _____

2. P: _____

 R: _____

UNIDAD 10

D.   You like to call people by their nicknames. What do you call your friends?
Use **-ito** or **-ita** to write each name.

[M] Rosa   **Rosita** _____

1. Juana _____   4. Roberto _____

2. Ana _____   5. Teresa _____

3. Miguel _____   6. Luis _____

E.   You use diminutive endings to talk about other things, too. How would you
change the following sentences? Write your answers on the lines.

[M]   1.   2.   3.   4.

[M] Mi abuela tiene dos conejos.   **Mi abuelita tiene dos conejitos.**

1. Mi prima lee un libro. _____

2. Hay tres gatos en la ventana. _____

3. El oso es un animal divertido. _____

4. Mi primo Jaime tiene un perro. _____

¿Cómo lo dices?   Nombre _____

F. What people and things are special to you? Write sentences about the special people, animals, or things in your world. Read Rosario's sentences below. Then use **-ito, -itos, -ita** or **-itas** to write your own five sentences.

1. Vivo en una casita pequeñita.
2. Tengo un amiguito. Él se llama Pablito.
3. Mi hermanita se llama Clarita.
4. En la clase de español escribo en mi cuadernito.
5. Me gustan mucho los perritos y las mariposita.

1. _____

2. _____

3. _____

4. _____

5. _____

THINK FAST! ∿∿∿∿∿∿∿∿∿∿∿∿∿∿∿∿

José is upset with his friend Alberto. Unscramble the words to find out what has happened.

¡ _____ tiene todos mis _____ , mis
       toAltiber   petoslipa

_____ y mis _____ !
   dertosnicua   tosbrili

UNIDAD 10

¿Cómo lo dices?　　　Nombre _____

¡APRENDE MÁS!

A suffix is a set of letters that you attach to the end of a word to give the word a different meaning. For example, the endings **-ito, -itos, -ita**, and **-itas** are suffixes. When you add them to the end of a word, you change the meaning to indicate smallness or affection.

Compare the following lists of words in Spanish and English:

Spanish		English	
rojo	roj**izo**	red	redd**ish**
el niño	la niñ**ez**	child	child**hood**
tonto	la tont**ería**	foolish	foolish**ness**
blanco	la blanc**ura**	white	white**ness**
el amigo	la amis**tad**	friend	friend**ship**
terrible	terrible**mente**	terrible	terrib**ly**

In each example, the meaning of the word changes because the suffix was added. When you know how suffixes work, you have a good clue to guessing the meanings of new words.

See how well you can spot a suffix. Read the following sentences and underline each word that you think has a suffix.

Me gusta la frescura de la mañana.　　　I like the coolness of the morning.

Diana aprende fácilmente.　　　Diana learns easily.

No me gusta la oscuridad de la noche.　　　I don't like the darkness of the night.

La verdura del verano es bella.　　　The greenness of summer is pretty.

Nombre _____

La página de diversiones

La sopa de letras

Find the secret words in the alphabet soup. Cross out the letters for each word in the lists. With the letters that are left, form the secret words.

papá	hermano	hijo	mamá	nieto
nieta	abuela	hermana	hija	abuelo

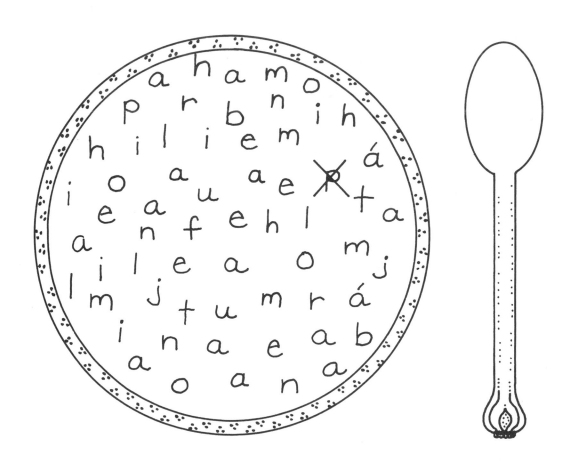

Las palabras secretas: ___ ___   ___ ___ ___ ___ ___ ___ ___ ___